Recruiting the Future of Medicine

recruiting the future of

MEDICINE

how to attract a
WORLD-CLASS
team

DAVID WOLFE

Published by Advantage, Charleston, South Carolina.
Member of Advantage Media Group.

ADVANTAGE is a registered trademark, and the Advantage colophon is a trademark of Advantage Media Group, Inc.

Printed in the United States of America.

10 9 8 7 6 5 4 3 2 1

ISBN: 978-1-64225-065-7
LCCN: 2018959339

Book design by Megan Elger.

This publication is designed to provide accurate and authoritative information in regard to the subject matter covered. It is sold with the understanding that the publisher is not engaged in rendering legal, accounting, or other professional services. If legal advice or other expert assistance is required, the services of a competent professional person should be sought.

Advantage Media Group is proud to be a part of the Tree Neutral® program. Tree Neutral offsets the number of trees consumed in the production and printing of this book by taking proactive steps such as planting trees in direct proportion to the number of trees used to print books. To learn more about Tree Neutral, please visit **www.treeneutral. com**.

Advantage Media Group is a publisher of business, self-improvement, and professional development books and online learning. We help entrepreneurs, business leaders, and professionals share their Stories, Passion, and Knowledge to help others Learn & Grow. Do you have a manuscript or book idea that you would like us to consider for publishing? Please visit **advantagefamily.com** or call **1.866.775.1696**.

TABLE OF CONTENTS

PART III: RETAINING "THE FUTURE WORKFORCE"

PREFACE

"Recruiting is the lifeblood of any program,
so you can't put anything above that."

—Pete Carroll, Head Football Coach
of the Seattle Seahawks

During my senior year of college, I knew I wanted to be a college baseball coach. I loved working with kids and seeing them achieve their dreams through a team. So before I began my journey into college coaching, I went to my college baseball coach, Clint Myers. Coach Myers has coached multiple national championship teams at Arizona State University and Central Arizona College. In a phone conversation, I asked him for his best advice as I entered into college coaching. To my surprise, he started to talk about recruiting. He went on and on about finding scouts and coaches you can trust to give you an honest evaluation of players. He talked about how to find these people and how to know whether you can trust their recommendation of players. This conversation went on for about thirty minutes.

Afterward, I was disappointed. I wanted to hear about how to teach hitting and pitching, when to call hits and runs and bunts, how to develop players, etc. I wanted to talk strategy and management. I thought, "Well that was a waste of time, I now know some stuff about recruiting, but that wasn't why I called him." A few years into college coaching, it started to sink in why he had talked so much about recruiting and not coaching. I realized if you want to win at a high level, you need the best players. It seems to me that about 90 percent of the time, the team with the better players wins the games; that's why it's so remarkable and publicized when a team with a lower skill level comes together as a unit and beats the better-skilled teams. Good coaches can develop players and make them better, but that takes a lot of time and is an art. I learned that if you want to win in college sports, then you want to spend a lot of time recruiting. And you need to be really good at it or you will lose games and lose your job. I learned that, in any organization, recruiting is priority number one; after

Recruiting needs to be priority #1 in any organization.

that, you can spend time developing them the best you can.

The workforce is changing and recruiting is changing. What worked years ago won't work in the future. We all hear that the business of healthcare is changing all the time. And it is. There is no doubt that the way we provide healthcare in this country, and how we pay for it, has undergone incredible transformation over the past decade. But something else has changed as well—how we attract the talent needed to make those changes work. The mindset of the future workforce is more different than anything prior. The traditional methods of interrogating talent doesn't work with this future workforce. The future workforce must be courted and attracted in addition to being vetted. Most organizations are heavily into vetting and interrogation, or they are really heavily relying on hiring fast and showing the candidate they are desperate for them. There must be a balance between selling and courting while you are vetting, so that if your candidates get an offer from you, they feel like they just got into Harvard (even when you only have one candidate to choose from).

Recruiting and attracting great people is becoming tougher and tougher. And attracting high-demand medical professionals will become even harder. What might have worked ten and twenty years ago doesn't work now. For one thing, there are fewer candidates. As of this writing, unemployment is low, and it's trickier to find good talent. Nurse Practitioners (NPs) have a 0.7 percent unemployment rate, significantly below the national average, coupled with a mean annual wage of $107,480 and median salary of $103,880 in 2017.[1]

More importantly, though, is the fact that the workforce of the future is changing. The number-one workforce demographic right now is millennials, those born between 1981 and 1996. Today's twenty- and thirty-somethings will, by the year 2025, make up 75 percent of the workforce.[2] And the way we attract, recruit, and vet them must be different than the way we recruited their parents or older siblings. We need to get inside of their heads, understand their hot buttons and what's important to them, and push

---

1   Bureau of Labor Statistics, "Nurse Anesthetists, Nurse Midwives, and Nurse Practitioners," *Occupational Outlook Handbook*, last modified April 13, 2018, www.bls.gov/ooh/ healthcare/nurse-anesthetists-nurse-midwives-and-nurse-practitioners.htm.

2   Debra Donston-Miller, "Workforce 2020: What You Need to Know," *Forbes* online, May 5 2016, https://www.forbes.com/ sites/workday/2016/05/05/workforce-2020-what-you-need-to-know-now/#78265b7e2d63..

those buttons to get the best of that group to come work for us.

That's why I am writing this book. I want to help our clients understand this new phase of recruiting (and attracting) in order to help them build "world-class" teams that give them a huge competitive advantage. In this book, I will cover how to attract the best available talent to your organization and how to grow and retain this future workforce.

I grew up in Tucson, Arizona, when my parents moved out there to be closer to my retiring grand-parents. As a kid, I was all about sports—baseball, football, and golf. My first real career out of college was coaching college baseball. It was my dream job—and it's how I got into the recruiting field. As a college coach at San Francisco State and Charleston Southern University, I spent long hours recruiting junior college and high school players throughout the state of California and the southeast. The job was great, but the pay and the hours were not. When our head coach at Charleston Southern left his position, all the assistant coaches lost theirs. So I went looking for a new coaching position. I got offered the pitching coach position at the University of Buffalo, New York. The obstacle to moving to New York was that my wife and I were expecting our first child in just two months, so I wasn't about to relocate with the birth being so close. I couldn't do it, and I am not sure if my wife would have followed me. So, because I heard good things about the recruiting field and had recruiting experience, I took a job with a large national Registered Nurse (RN) staffing company and learned the business.

I did that for two years, and then left for a healthcare recruiting company out of Tennessee. I started a new line of business for them, focusing on psychiatric Nurse Practitioner permanent placements. That became very successful, but I wanted to place all types of NPs and saw a huge need for quality NP permanent recruiting services. There was a big need for good permanent placements NP firms, so I decided to take my life savings (with two kids and one on the way) and go into business myself. My vision was to be the absolute best source for healthcare groups to find permanent NPs and Physician Assistants (PAs).

The workforce is changing and recruiting is changing. What worked years ago won't work in the future.

I'm entrepreneurial by nature. I've been starting businesses since I was nine years old. I saw the Nurse Practitioner niche as an opportunity to really help the marketplace. I had dabbled in recruiting other medical professions but I firmly believed that NPs and PAs are the future of medicine.

Most of the competitors in the space were just doing temporary staffing or short-term assignments. And the companies that were doing permanent NPs and PAs weren't supplying medical centers with quality providers. They weren't really listening to clients, and they weren't sending candidates who met the requirements. So I launched my company—NP Now—in 2012. We started focusing on less-densely populated areas where the demand for permanent NPs was greatest. Our clients were telling us, "If you can find me a Nurse Practitioner, you can save our clinic. You can help our patients get better healthcare faster. They won't have to drive hours to the nearest big city to get care."

By 2016, through email exchanges with the United States Bureau of Labor Statistics, we learned we had become the number-one NP search firm in the US for permanent placements. Through lots of trial and error in the healthcare recruiting space, I built what I believe to be the most effective ways to recruit and retain top talent.

My goal is for you to apply these methods so you can build your own world-class team. That will help your business to become more profitable, improve the company culture, make it a better place to work, boost patient satisfaction scores, and improve the health of your community.

What's at Stake

For healthcare recruiters, the timing could not be more critical. According to the *US News and World Report*'s "Best Job Rankings," Nurse Practitioners hold the number-two spot in terms of the best one hundred occupations in the United States.[3] (RNs, by the way, are number twenty-two.) With the shortage of primary care MDs, the demand for NPs is higher than the demand for MDs.

As states change laws regarding advanced practice registered nurses, NPs are becoming more widely utilized as a source for primary healthcare, says the US Bureau of Labor Statistics (BLS). In fact, the BLS reports a whopping 31 percent job growth rate

---

3   "The 100 Best Jobs," *U.S. News and World Report*, accessed 2018, https://money.usnews.com/careers/best-jobs/rankings/the-100-best-jobs.

through 2026 for Nurse Practitioners, and estimates that some forty-four thousand job openings in the field will occur.[4] Considering that the average job growth rate for all other occupations combined is 7 percent for the same time period, the prospects for NPs is forecast to be excellent, especially for those choosing to practice in large inner cities or in remote rural areas, where medical doctors and healthcare treatment are at a premium. In other words, for every one engineering job, sales position, or accounting job open, there will be four NP jobs open.

But NPs, PAs, and RNs were in the top twenty-five hardest-to-fill occupations in the healthcare sector of the staffing industry in the fourth quarter of 2017, according to the American Staffing Association (ASA) Skills Gap Index.[5] By 2030, ninety thousand MDs will be retiring and there will be only sixty-eight thousand NPs to fill that void, making the demand even higher.

It's important to factor in that as the demand for these providers go up, so does the time it takes

---

4   Bureau of Labor Statistics, "Nurse Anesthetists, Nurse Midwives, and Nurse Practitioners."

5   American Staffing Association, "ASA Skills Gap Index," *ASA*, accessed 2018, https://americanstaffing.net/ staffing-research-data/asa-staffing-industry-data/ asa-skills-gap-index/.

to fill these types of openings. It's a big factor that most groups don't always consciously consider. At NP Now, we calculated the cost of vacancy for an NP or PA at between $68,182 and $90,682 per month. And the cost increases each month as it takes the organization longer into the search. In addition, the lost revenue (which is different from the cost of vacancy) for a position open ninety days is $110,880. NPs on average generate $70 per patient and see about twenty-four patients per day, equaling about $1,680/day, and there are 220 working days per year.

It's vital to attract the right people, and you may only get one shot. You can't afford to be poor at selling your company and telling your story. NPs and other sought-after medical professionals have so many options, and their options are only going to get better. Most of the time, they are getting multiple offers while they are interviewing. They will only choose the companies that are doing great things and that articulate that in the recruiting process. It's up to you to attract them to you. I'm here to show you how to succeed.

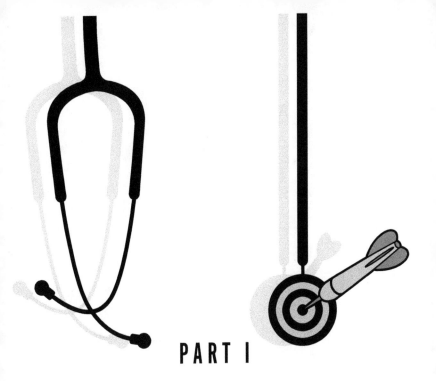

PART I

Attraction-Based Recruiting

CHAPTER 1

People Want to Join Winning Organizations

In the standard model of recruiting, the employer posts a job opening. It includes two parts. Part one essentially says, "Here's what the job duties are." Part two says, "Here's what's required of the candidate in order to do the job." It's essentially all about the employer.

What's in it for the candidate? Why would the candidate even be interested?

That, in a nutshell, is what makes attraction-based recruiting different.

In attraction-based recruiting, you make it about the candidate. You make the candidate want to come work for you. You do that by telling your story, and telling it really well. What I mean by this is just as simple as answering some easy questions: Where did your company come from? How big were you ten years ago, twenty years ago? Where is your company going? Why should someone be interested in working for your company?

WHAT IS ATTRACTION-BASED RECRUITING?

There are three parts to attraction-based recruiting.

First, attraction-based recruiting is **appealing to the candidate's unique hot buttons or pain points, and telling and positioning your story in a way that inspires and excites someone you are recruiting.** It's putting yourself in their shoes and thinking, "What would I be looking for in a new group if I were looking for a new position? What would I want?" It's telling your company's story in a way that hits on as many of what are known as the Five Prime Motivators as possible.

The Five Prime Motivators are those hot buttons and pain points that candidates look for and carry with them from one place of employment to another. They were determined by our coach, Greg Doersching, and are outlined below:

1. Work-life balance. More time with loved ones

2. Ego. This position sounds prestigious. I would be proud to tell others what I do, and I am good at this.

3. Growth. The position offers a way to advance skills and improve career trajectory.

4. Proximity to loved ones. They want to be close to home.

5. Money. Typically, people make a 5–10 percent increase in base salary when they take a new position. If they stay in their current job, on average people received a 2–3 percent increase each year.

We'll talk more about the Five Prime Motivators later on in chapter 3, but before we get there, you need to learn a little more about attraction-based recruiting, which is directly related. Attraction-based recruiting is listening closely to why candidates are looking for a new position and what they see in your opportunity—and selling to that. You will only be able to get these truths from your recruit if they can let their guard down enough to trust you. Build rapport so that they know you care about them more than you care about what they can do for you. They will open up to you and be candid about why they are seeking a new position and what makes your position attractive.

Attraction-based recruiting is courting candidates and recruiting them based on the information they have given you. It shows that you are really listening and you really care, and people want to join organizations where leadership cares about them and hears them. People respond more openly to others when they can tell that you care.

Attraction-based recruiting draws in candidates by telling your company's unique story. Growth, mentorship, voice, purpose—these are the qualities that motivate today's future workforce. Attraction-based recruiting gives these candidates a clear picture of your company's past and present, and outlines their place and purpose in its forward trajectory. Candidates are attracted to winning organizations, especially when they can envision their role in your company's success.

The second part to attraction-based recruiting is building a relationship and a connection. Put yourself out there. No one cares what you have to say unless they first know that you care about them. The more you connect with the candidate and build a relationship during the recruiting process, the much more likely they are to pick your company over another. At the end of the recruiting process, they are going to ask themselves, "Who wants me more and who cares about me more?"

Third, attraction-based recruiting is painting the picture to the candidate of where you see them going in your organization. Tell them specifically where you see them going and what role you see them playing in five to ten years. This will motivate someone more than you can imagine, plus, it shows you care enough and have enough foresight to look after their future, which no one else is doing that for them—almost guaranteed.

Later in the book, I will go over how to create an attraction-based job description

(ABJD) and use it as a tool to attract and recruit (and tell your story).[6]

The big premise here is that people want to join what they perceive to be winning teams. Everybody wants to be a part of a winning team, especially the younger workforce. They want to get behind a grand purpose, something bigger than themselves. What is attractive to this younger workforce is seeing that a company is going in some really cool direction and they're doing some really big things.

I learned this when I was a baseball coach. I coached at San Francisco State University and Charleston Southern University, both smaller schools. When we were recruiting athletes that we wanted to play on our team, I found that nine out of ten times they always chose the bigger school with the bigger name in the bigger conference. They chose the Pac-12 school or the SEC school—even though they knew they weren't going to play in the games right away. They might sit on the bench for two or three years, whereas at our school they could start as

---

6   Like the Five Prime Motivators, the ABJD was created by Coach Greg Doersching, who received the lifetime achievement award in recruiting in 2017 from NAPS (National Association of Personnel Services).

a freshman and make a big impact right then. And yet, nine out of ten would choose the bigger school, like Stanford, University of Texas or University of Florida. Why? Because of the image and the perception of being on a winning team.

It's human nature to want to join the team with the bigger and better image. That's why, in business, telling your story is so important. Not only where you are now, but also where you came from and where you're going. More importantly, how are you winning? What are the metrics that show how you're winning? What is uncommon about you? What is your vision for continued winning in the future? Again, attraction is the key to recruiting, especially with the future workforce.

Can You Tell Your Group's Story Really Well?

We ask hiring managers, what are the top two to three selling points about your group that would entice someone to leave their job and come work for you? Why did you join the group and why do you stay?

We usually hear something like this: "We are a great place to work. We have been around for a while. We have good tenure." Or, "We have good medical benefits and everyone is laid back." The problem with these is there are no specifics, just general statements like "great" and "good." And the answers are too short. Thus, it may seem like the group doesn't have much to offer. About 90 percent of the groups we interview sell their story like this. If you are a high-performing A-player, would you want to join this type of company?

When telling your company's story, you must touch on four things:

1. Where your group came from. (Be specific, for example, the year founded, number of locations, number of people on the team, etc.)

2. Where your group is going. (Your vision. Be specific. What exactly are you trying to accomplish in the next five to ten years? What is your core purpose?)

3. Why this role is vital to the success of your organization.

4. How you value and appreciate your team. (Again, be specific.)

TWO EXAMPLES OF TELLING A COMPANY'S STORY WELL

- "One of our top clients is seeking a family Nurse Practitioner to work full-time in a primary care setting. They are among the nation's leading providers for employer-based health services. They were founded in 2005 by Richard Tarrant with the vision that wellness needs to be as much about the well as the unwell. They are based in Vermont and are in forty states and several industries, such as finance, school districts, and manufacturing. One of the things I love about this company is that they keep their mission at the forefront of all they do, and that mission is to improve their population's health by identifying health risks and working with people one-on-one to help mitigate those risks. They do this through thirty-minute visits with every patient—at a minimum! (And we know this is sometimes hard to find in health-care these days.) They emphasize health coaching to support individual lifestyle changes and health outcomes within their patients, and they have their own proprietary EMR, which enables them to truly see health progression in the patients they serve. They've recently been ranked by *Modern Health* as one of the best places to work in the country, because of the way they value and appreciate their providers through programs that offer regular recognition, education, and support. And they give all their employees a platform to bring new ideas to the table and implement growth. Their core purpose is to put health back into healthcare."

- "David Wolfe, founder and CEO, started NP Now in 2012 in order to meet a basic need in the market for quality NP permanent placement services. David saw that there were a lot of recruiters doing poor-quality work, and health systems needed better service on the permanent NP recruiting side. David started NP Now with one part-time marketing person (Monica, who is still with the company) after he took all of his savings from the earnings from his previous recruiting position. Each year the company has grown in revenue 30–50 percent, and now they serve close to five hundred health systems. In 2016, they became the number-one NP search firm in the United States for permanent placements, according to the United States Bureau of Labor Statistics.[7] The company's ten-year vision is to place six hundred NPs and PAs per year in new, permanent positions by 2027. They truly live out their three core values: 'We deliver, we serve, and we get better every day.' It's not something they just say. Their core purpose and why they do what they do is: 'We connect people to improve life.' Everybody on the NP Now team acts like they own the company; they are all extremely invested because they have a voice in how things are done and they really care about the overall

---

7   Bureau of Labor Statistics, "Nurse Anesthetists, Nurse Midwives, and Nurse Practitioners."

service they provide. The new recruiter role will play a big impact in the growth of the company by helping the company find NPs for our clients that they had no hope in finding on their own."

It Takes Vision

"Where there is no vision, the people perish..."
—Proverbs 29:18

The first, and most important part of attraction-based recruiting, is the ten-year vision of the company. Where are you going in the next ten years? People will rally behind that, if it's big enough. If that means you want to grow from serving x number of patients in your community to three times that in ten years, or if you want to grow revenue from y amount to x amount, be specific. Make it a metric, and emphasize how that positively affects the community, the team, the group, the company culture, and all the other areas that people can get behind and support.

The truth is that most organizations do not have a clear vision. If people can't see the vision, if they can't see where they're going, it reduces morale, it reduces motivation, and people don't really want to join groups like that.

Examples of typical vision statements for a healthcare organization include, "Be recognized as the preferred health system in the county." Or, "Change the face of healthcare." Or, "Enhance the delivery of healthcare." These visions are too vague. How does someone know if they are really accomplishing the vision? If it's not defined—*how* will you change the face of healthcare?—then how does the group know they are winning?

NPs and other providers are used to seeing these types of visions all the time. My recommendation is to come up with a vision that is measurable and big, and set it for ten years out. That's something people will get behind and become passionate about. Something like, "We want to serve and treat ten thousand patients in our community in 2028." Or, "In ten years, we want to go from five locations to fifteen locations and provide healthcare in three counties instead of one, improving the lives of sixty-five thousand people." Or, "We want our patient satisfaction scores to go from 5.6 to 9.0 by 2028 and to make the people in our community 60 percent healthier." The goal needs to be a bit of a stretch but big enough to inspire your team to hustle and excite them to come to work every day.

The second most important part of attraction-based recruiting is core values. Those are things that are actually lived out and are alive within a company. That's how the company operates. What are the three to five biggest values that the company lives by? They are important, because you hire by them, and you retain people by them. These core values need to come to life. Most organizations have mission statements and core values, but they really don't mean anything to anybody.

Values can include philanthropy, but this is not required; it is just an add-on. For instance, we donate a percentage of our profit to Water Mission. Water Mission provides sustainable clean water across the world. And, for example, if we donated $16,000, we would directly save 533 lives. When we can see this impact, it makes a difference in the work we do. This future workforce is really getting behind that. They want to join companies with a clear vision and strong core values, because it makes them feel like they're a part of something bigger than themselves.

The core purpose is very important: Why you do what you do? This isn't a mission statement; it is how you are making an impact. The Disney Company's core purpose is, "We make people happy." Our core purpose at NP Now is, "We connect people to improve life."

As a healthcare organization, what is your core purpose? You want your core purpose to be so big that even after somebody retires, they would still come back and volunteer with your organization, because they believe in your purpose so much. That's extremely idealistic. It's not very probable. But that's the idea behind creating a strong core purpose, and the future workforce is really looking for that strong core purpose.

> **You want your core purpose to be so big that even after somebody retires, they would still come back and volunteer with your organization, because they believe in your purpose so much.**

Along with telling your story, attraction-based recruiting should focus on why the position is open, and then how the new team member can be a catalyst and make a huge impact in the group. You've told the story, so now how do they fit in within your company's growth story? It's talking about how this role that you're recruiting them for is vital to the big picture of the organization. You don't want to present some sort of big vision and then say, "Hey, you're only going to be doing this over here, and it doesn't really matter." You are clearly explaining, "This is what we're doing, and this is how this new role is going to make a big impact within the organization. If we select you, here's how you would make a big impact within the organization."

You want them to feel like they're a catalyst, an agent for powerful change, a part of something big.

We Eat Our Own Food

"Culture eats strategy for breakfast."

—Peter Drucker

I have applied the theories I just presented to our own internal hiring and had great success with them. We have 100 percent retention with a staff made up entirely of millennials. They have made us a fast-growing company that became the number-one Nurse Practitioner search firm in the United States in 2016. We grow at a rate of 30 to 50 percent a year. And I say that because we're not taking just anybody; we only want the people who really hustle and who are really bright. We have a high standard, and we have an excellent retention rate because we bring people through this hiring process.

Here's our story, our core vision, and our core purpose. In Jim Collins's book *Good to Great*, he talks about creating a Big Hairy Audacious Goal—a BHAG. Our BHAG, our ten-year vision, is that we want to place six hundred NPs and PAs per year in new, permanent positions by 2027. That means in 2027 we know that we will be improving the lives of close three million patients.

Our three core values are: "We deliver, we serve, and we get better every day." We hire and retain based on those three things. When we hire, we ask ourselves, does this person seem like they fit our company culture? Do they deliver, do they hustle, do they run through obstacles to serve, and do they care about people more than about the bottom line? Are they improving every day? What's the one thing we can all do each day to get incrementally better at what we're doing?

Our core purpose is: "We connect people to improve life." When we supply medical centers with Nurse Practitioners, we're improving the Nurse Practitioners' lives by finding them better jobs, and we're improving hiring managers' lives by finding them top-notch Nurse Practitioners who make their company better and wealthier and improve patient outcome scores. How does this core purpose play out logistically? As an example, if we place one hundred NPs and PAs, we know we improved the lives of 480,000 patients a year. This was based off the fact the average NP sees about twenty-four patients per day and works forty-eight weeks of the year.

Our core values, our core purpose, and our vision, or BHAG, are very much alive within the organization. Everybody on the team rallies behind those three things. It's not just something that we say. It's something that we do, live by, and grade ourselves on. At the end of each quarter, we present a core value award. We all vote on the person who we think most exemplified a core value, which core value they exemplified, and how they exemplified that core value. It's a way for us to show that we're living out our core values, and that we're taking them seriously.

A key facet to building these core values and purpose is to have your team (every employee) make them. That's how we did it. The level of buy-in increases drastically if the people on the team have a voice in making them. If the leader of an organization just says, "Here are our core values, and here's our vision," it doesn't carry as much meaning. When we did it, we had offsite meetings to discuss what we wanted our values and purpose to be. It took a lot of time, and we argued over it, but in the end, we grinded through it to figure out our vision, values, and purpose. That's what gets the buy-in.

The bigger you can make that group of employees, the better. If you're a twenty-person company, make it everybody in the company. If you're a fifty-person company, maybe make it only ten or fifteen people, but then get everybody else's voice. Let them at least have an opinion on it, and then the buy-in will follow.

A great place to start creating your core values is with Simon Sinek, whose book and YouTube video cover his message, "Start with Why." That's how we created our "why" and our core purpose of connecting people to improve lives. I suggest you have your team watch that hour-long video and read his book. He explains how a team can come up with a core purpose that comes alive and thrives within an organization.

It's the same thing with core values. The questions in creating core values are: What are the three to five things that your company is strongest at? What are the principles you live by? What are the principles that you will hire and fire based off, and if people consistently do not live up to one of these core values, would be grounds for them no longer being on the team?

The other way to figure out how to create core values is if everybody on the team were to go start another business, what are the three to five things that they would do in that business that you're currently doing? If you were to go start an ice cream shop, what are those three values that you're going to live by, you're going to hire by, and you're going to keep as the benchmark? As I said, our three are we deliver—which means that we hustle, we focus on results and getting it done for our clients—we serve, and we get better every day. If we started another company, we would still live by those three values, no matter what we did. I think getting everybody's input and everybody's voice has a big impact when creating those.

CHAPTER 2

Why You Need to Attract "A" Players— and Only "A" Players

"The toughest decisions in organizations are people decisions—hiring, firing, and promoting people. These are the decisions that receive the least attention and are the ones that are the hardest to 'unmake.'"

—Peter Drucker

In 2016, an outpatient mental health group outside Baltimore had just hired an NP who interviewed extremely well and said all the right things during the interview. After just a few weeks, this NP proved to be mean and nasty. Patients refused to come to the clinic and gave the group bad reviews online. The NP drove co-workers crazy, to the point that they said, "She needs to leave or we are leaving." At this point, the practice administrator contacted us and told us the situation. We let her know there were better NPs out there that we could land for her. She then felt empowered to terminate this NP and have us do the search. We filled the position three weeks later. This can happen easily, and it happens often when groups are inconsistent and not thorough in their hiring process. They often end up with the wrong players on their team.

Let's talk about the players you want to recruit for your team. I divide players into three categories: A, B, and C. In the simplest terms:

- A-players are people who exceeds your expectations. They bring more value to your team than their total compensation.

- B-Players are people who meets requirements about 70 percent of the time.

- C-Players are people who only meet expectations about 30 percent of the time. Most of the time they are falling short of minimum requirements.

The key to success is being vigilant at hiring only A-players. Or, as importantly, when hiring younger workers who haven't had the time to establish themselves as A-players, getting B-players who can be coached into A-players.

What percentage of your hires have been A-players? According to *Avoid Costly Mis-Hires!* By Dr. Bradford Smart, statistically, only 25 percent of all hires are high performers. He also said that 50 percent of hires are mis-hires.

The goal is to get that A-player percentage as high as possible. In a perfect world, we would all love having eight out of ten hires being or turning into A-players. But I think that's unrealistic, especially with this future workforce. With them, a more realistic target is hiring 40 percent A-players, and then making sure that the other 60 percent are B-players with the majority of them showing signs that—given the right tools, resources, and mentorship—they can grow and develop into A-players.

If you can get that ratio of 40 percent or even 50 percent A-players and the rest promising B-players, then you will greatly improve your company's success. In this difficult recruiting and employment landscape, that's important. Because it's a younger workforce, they need to be trained and mentored into the A-player category. While you're going to shoot for the A-player, what needs to happen more often is hiring somebody who is a B-player, who meets the requirements about 70 percent of the time, but who, with training over the course of two to five years, will likely become an A-player.

I believe you must incorporate into the recruiting and hiring equation talking about how you develop your team members. Organizations across most all fields spend about 40 to 80 percent of their money on people (salary, employee benefits, PTO, etc), but they spend only about 1 percent on training and ongoing development.[8] If companies can find good people, and if they focus on mentoring and training, they can turn those B-players into A-players.

The good news is that this future workforce really does want training. They want to learn. They want constant feedback, they want clear expectations, and they want to be held accountable. I think account-ability has been lost in the workforce. Sometime in the last ten or twenty years, it has become uncool to hold people accountable. But this younger workforce actually responds well to accountability, and they want it. They want to know where they stand and how they can improve their skills. Giving that to them is important. It helps them turn into A-players,

---

8   Carol Deeb, "Percent of a Business Budet for Salary," Chron, https://smallbusiness.chron.com/percent-business-budget-salary-14254.html.

which your organization needs in this highly competitive environment.

The High Cost of C-Players

You notice I haven't even mentioned C-players yet. That's because you need to avoid C-players at all costs. In fact, cost is the reason. Hiring a C-player will cost you massive amounts of money.

Dr. Bradford Smart says one out of every two hires in the US is a mis-hire.[9] What is a mis-hire? It's when a new hire fails to meet the desired results within their first year in their position. That's pretty much the definition of a C-player.

According to Dr. Brad Smart, who leads the recruiting organization Topgrading, a mis-hire will cost the organization somewhere between five and twenty-four times

A mis-hire will cost the organization somewhere between five and twenty-four times the annual salary of that position.

9   Bradford Smart, "The Game-Changing Magic of Hiring
     A-Players for Your Organization," Growth Institute, https://
     blog.growthinstitute.com/topgrading/a-players.

the annual salary of that position.[10] Think about that for a minute. If a new hire has a base compensation at $102,692, then the net average cost of a mis-hire is $1,502,436 (14.6 times base compensation, plus opportunity costs, hiring fees, stress on other staff, lost revenue, etc.). For Nurse Practitioners, I calculated that at a cost of $830,239.12 for every mis-hire. Based on this, even hiring a B-player can be costly. The total cost of hiring a B-Player versus an A-player equates to $311,567.98 for an NP or PA.

The cost to your company in hiring the wrong person goes far beyond just the dollars. Consider the cost to your current staff, in terms of the stress caused by a mis-hire. Or consider how a mis-hire might actually cause you to lose patients. I have heard many stories of candidates presenting themselves well during the interview, being well spoken, and saying all the right things. But once they got hired and settled into the position, they were the exact opposite of how they presented themselves. They were a jerk to the staff. Worst of all, they were horrible with patients. I've heard many stories from smaller practice groups that really took a big hit and lost a sizable portion of

---

10   Bradford Smart, "Topgrading 201: How to Avoid Costly Mis-Hires," 2012, https://topgrading.com/_tg-content/downloads/Topgrading-eBook.pdf.

their patients just because this one bad practitioner got in front of too many people before they figured out what the practitioner was doing. It takes a period of time, perhaps several months or even years, before you might get the feedback from patients and staff that lets you see what impact this mis-hire is having and how detrimental this person is to the whole organization and to the brand.

This is especially true in this age of constant ratings on the Internet and the need to keep patient satisfaction scores high. If a patient has a bad experience with a Nurse Practitioner or physician, you can bet that he or she is going to write about it on Yelp, Google, or on their Facebook page. Can you afford that kind of bad publicity?

"Nothing matters more in winning than getting the right people on the field," Jack Welch once said. "All the clever strategies and advanced technologies in the world are nowhere near as effective without great people to put them to work."[11]

Jack Welch employed all of these methods we are about to talk about when he grew GE in the 1980s and 1990s. He went from hiring 20 percent A-players to 80 percent in three years using these

---

11   Jack Welch, with Suzy Welch, *Winning: The Ultimate Business How-To Book* (New York: HarperCollins, 2009).

methods. Because of this, GE went from a $1.5 billion company to a $130 billion company.

Imagine if you were hiring 80 percent A-players. What would that do for you, your patients, your community, and your organization?

Separating the A-players from the Rest

As a recruiter, your job is to find your organization A-players and to weed out the under-performers, the C-players. Now, no one admits to being a C-player. Everyone presents himself or herself in the best possible light. For some, that may mean fabricating, exaggerating, or out-and-out lying on their résumés. In fact, according to HireRight's 2017 employment screening benchmark report, 85 percent of employers caught applicants lying on their resumes or applications, up from just 66 percent five years ago.[12] For others, it may mean they are master interviewers, but they really don't have a lot of substance. In both cases, there's a lot of fluff. There's a lot of talk, but there's not real substance, and there's not a real history of success.

In my nine-step hiring process, you will greatly increase your chances to be able to sniff out those

---

12 "2018 Employment Screening Benchmarking Report," *HireRight*, www.hireright.com/benchmarking.

kinds of fakers and fabricators and find the candidates who truly are or can be A-players.

It starts by telling your company's story powerfully and hitting as many of the candidates' hot buttons/pain points and prime motivators as possible. A-players will become attracted to that, because they're going to see what's going on within the company, and they're going to be attracted to the right things. That's part of the vetting process: listening to hear what parts of your story they are attracted to.

For instance, if they're only attracted to areas like your compensation, your benefits, and your paid time off, then those are probably a bit of a red flag. Those factors, though they are certainly important, should not be any candidate's prime motivator—certainly not an A-player candidate. But if you ask them why they applied to your company and why they're interested in joining your team, and they start talking about things like how they love your ten-year vision, how you live out your core values, how inspiring your core purposes is, and all the great things you're doing in the community, then that's a far better sign. It's one indicator that this person might be an A-player.

As I said, A-players are attracted to companies that are winning and companies that are filled with other A-players. That's often because they are winners themselves. One of the most important signals that someone is an A-player is that they are already a high performer. They have a history of success somewhere in their background. Whatever they did, whether it's in sports, or in school, or at another job, or a hobby, whatever they've done in their life, they can show you some measure of success. Or they can demonstrate how they had to apply themselves—and put themselves at the risk of failing—in order to go after something that was hard and getting it. I think that's one of the biggest indicators of an A-player. They've been successful in many if not most of the things that they've done, and they can prove it.

> **A-players are attracted to companies that are winning and companies that are filled with other A-players.**

With that background, they're going to be attracted to a company that's also growing and doing big things and achieving success. Companies that tell their story really well and have a big vision tend to attract those A-players, and it tends to be a better match. And it can also weed out the Bs and Cs. Some of the lower performers are going to feel pressure. They may think, either consciously or subconsciously, "Hey, I'm going to be exposed here. If I apply and try to come into an organization that is doing all these things, it's just a matter of time before they will find out. I can only fake it so long."

The Nine-Step Recruiting Process to Hiring A-players and Building a World-Class Team

I have been studying the greatest recruiting and hiring experts, including Dave Ramsey, Jim Collins, Patrick Lencioni, and Bradford Smart, for many years now. As you'll see and learn more about in the next section, have distilled and synthesized their work and the work of others with my own personal experience to create a nine-step recruiting process for attraction-based recruiting. I use it to attract Nurse Practitioners and physician assistants for our clients (and to build my NP Now team), but there is no reason it cannot work for other positions in healthcare or in other industries.

This system is pretty comprehensive, and it covers most of the bases so that no mis-hires slip through the cracks and get through the door. It's designed to keep "crazy" out of your building. It's designed to expose the people who are faking and fabricating things. And it's designed to make it obvious who is a top performer, who is really going to fit into your company culture, and who's going to exemplify your core values.

It's also meant to be consistent, so that each candidate goes through this process so that you can easily compare one candidate to the next. One problem I see with other hiring systems is that a hiring manager may not be following consistent steps with each candidate. They cover five steps with one candidate and only three steps with the next candidate. If you follow my comprehensive nine-step process, you will find the A-players you need to succeed.

It's not bulletproof. Nothing is. It's inevitable that bad hires are going to be present in any organization. The goal is to reduce bad hires to the smallest percent possible. But I believe it gives you the best chance at hiring only a top performer that really fits into your company culture.

If you need help understanding or establishing any of these, or for more

information, come to me. I can help you formulate your attraction-based recruiting plan. You can reach me at david@npnow.com.

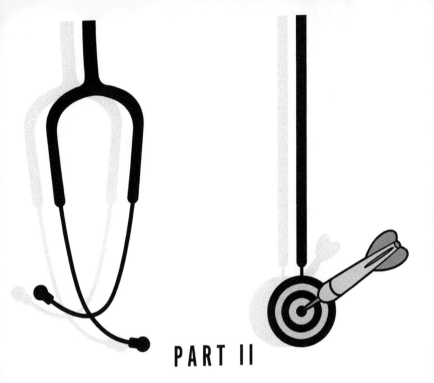

PART II

THE NINE-STEP RECRUITING AND HIRING PROCESS

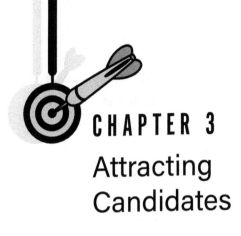

CHAPTER 3
Attracting Candidates

The following process has come about through a lot of trial and error recruiting NPs and PAs. I have seen what works, what's really sticky, what has the most power, and how to make sure the process focuses on what's in it for the candidate.

The process is meant to make the most of your recruiting time. It will help you not only find the right candidate for a current opening but will also let you build an organization of talent that will let you find perfect matches in the future. The goal is to get the best provider available at the time. By following my process, you will build a steady pipeline of talent so that whenever you have an opening, you will be able to locate stellar candidates and find that perfect match.

Remember, consistency is key. You need to follow all nine steps, in this order, to achieve the results you need to compete in today's recruiting environment.

The premise in starting a recruiting process is to cast a very wide net in effort to attract as many qualified people to your opening or organization as you can. You do this by attracting candidates as many ways as possible at your disposal. ***You must attract first***, qualify second. Most recruiters qualify first, this is a mistake. You want thirty people interested, so you can interview, vet and hand pick the best two or three out of the thirty. The other big premise in starting the recruiting process is you want to get your ABJD to as many connectors as possible because then you will have a multiplier effect because each connector may know fifty to one hundred other qualified people. This drastically improves your recruiting effectiveness.

STEP ONE: RECRUIT CANDIDATES

Finding candidates is the first job of any recruiter, and what follows is my six-point plan for attracting the best candidates out there.

First: Five Ways to Write an Attraction-Based Job Description

Telling your company's story better than anyone else is the beginning to landing A-players. Tell them where your group came from and where your group is going. People want to join what they perceive to be winning teams. Describe your ten-year vision, core values, and core purpose (why you do what you do). This isn't just a mission statement, it's a true story that is meant to attract people to you.

People are attracted to details, not generalities.

Explain why a new team member is needed. Describe how the new team member can be a catalyst and make a huge impact in the group's overall success. Everyone wants to feel like they are a part of something bigger than themselves.

I have included examples of good attraction-based job descriptions (ABJDs) in the appendix, and here is what each of them has in common:

1. **Be specific.** People are attracted to specifics, not generalities. Write about when you were founded, what awards you have won, your locations, the number of team members, their average tenure, the average time to get promoted or a raise. This makes your company and job seem real and candid.

2. **Tell how a candidate will fit into the story.** Tell them how they will make a big impact. Tell about why the position is open, where the company is going in the future, and how valuable this specific role is to the future of the company. Also, tell your core purpose—why you do what you do. The best candidates will be most attracted to your vision, core values, and core purpose, and these are likely to be your A-players.

3. **Show in detail how you value and appreciate your team members.** (Don't call them employees.) In addition to talking about 401(k) amounts and PTO time, talk about all the little things you do for your team members—birthday lunches, gifts to their favorite charity, turkeys on Thanksgiving, onsite daycare, award recognition, fun team outings, etc. A lot of people are leaving positions because they don't feel valued and appreciated.

4. **Include a salary range and bonus range, if it exists.** We have found through testing that more people will apply when there's

a salary range. If you offer productivity bonuses, sell it! Nothing excites a high performer more than a chance to be rewarded for high performance.

5. **Create an attractive headline on top of your ABJD that tells who you are, where you are and what you are looking for all in one sentence.** Include your name, email, and phone number in the top-right of the posting. People's eyes tend to move to the top-right. Don't put it at the bottom. You'll actually increase your applications by putting it at the top-right.

It doesn't have to be five thousand words long. You want it all to fit in an eight-by-eleven Word document sheet, at eleven- or twelve-point font. It's okay to use bullet points so it's easy to understand.

Second: Spread the Word That You Are Looking

You can easily multiply your efforts by finding the right people to help you recruit. Talk to twenty "connectors" and twenty A-players (also called "thoroughbreds") about what you are looking for and ask them for help. Connectors are people you know in the business who know a lot of other people. As for the other A-players, thoroughbreds run with other thoroughbreds, so contact other A-players. A-players are way more likely to know other high performers. Get the ABJD into their hands and tell them to go find as many as they can. A-players typically know other A-players.

Consider sweetening the pot with these people. Many recruiters offer small referral bonuses of $300 or $500. Think about boosting that to $3,000 or $5,000. If you can, you'll find those twenty A-players and twenty connectors will do some proactive recruiting for you. When you think about the cost of a job vacancy being anywhere from $63,000 to $93,000 a month, it may be worth it to offer a larger incentive to those connectors and A-players.

Third: Contact State, Local, and Educational Organizations

Get the ABJD into the hands of the local dean of the medical program you are recruiting for or the head of out-placement and ask them to pass it along to new grads or post-grads. Those are highly connected people who know the exact type of person you're recruiting. Also contact state and local organizations for whatever position you are filling. A Google search will find them; go to their website, call, or email them and find the person who can pass the posting out at their next meeting.

Fourth: Contact Previous Applicants

You should be keeping an internal database of candidates who have previously applied and/or are in your area. Maybe they weren't a fit for a position a year ago, but now they are. Or maybe you didn't have an opening for them three years ago, but now you do. You should stay in touch with them via newsletter, email, or content marketing to stay in front of them. Then, when a position opens, go right into your database and send them your attractive job description. Ask them if they're interested—or, if not, ask if they can pass it on.

Fifth: Cold Call

Professional organizations like medical or nursing boards have lists of all their members in their particular region. If you are in Boston, for example, you can get the names of everyone in the organization in a fifty-mile radius of Boston. These people may not have applied, so this is actual, real recruiting. Most everybody avoids this, because nobody likes cold calling, and it's a time-consuming task. (That's one of the reasons companies pay us to do it.) But it can be extremely effective. Just ask them for a couple minutes of their time to help you. Then tell your story and ask them if they want more information on it, or if they would be willing to pass your name along to a friend.

The fact is, this is where the real A-players are. They are happy where they are, they're doing a great job for their current employer, and they are not out on job boards looking for something else. This step is the hardest, but it can be the most fruitful step, because the candidates that apply to jobs on job boards are typically always on job boards, and they turn over in positions faster. They don't stay in positions as long, which is not what you want.

Sixth: Post the Job on Multiple Websites

Okay, I just said candidates on job boards may not be the best candidates. So why bother with them? Because at this stage of the process, you are casting as wide a net as possible. We have more than three hundred different online advertisement partners, just because we love the theory of casting a wide net, and there is a chance that we could hook somebody really good from a job board. I want to see all the candidates so I can evaluate them. A lot of healthcare groups rely only on candidates applying to their job; this is a big mistake if you want to build a world-class team.

STEP TWO: PHONE INTERVIEW

You've looked over the candidates, and you have narrowed them down to a handful who have most of the qualifications that you want. It's worth talking to them on the phone. Now comes the initial step of the screening process.

There are two questions that I recommend asking:

First: "What was most compelling about the job description that made you apply?"

In asking this, you're trying to learn what popped out to them. What is motivating them? You're trying to find out if they have good initial motivators or bad initial motivators.

If they answer that question in a way that's all about them, or what the job is going to give them, then that goes in the bad initial motivator bucket. If they talk about salary, PTO, and benefits up front, that's the bad bucket.

The good bucket holds answers such as, "I really like your story, I like your mission, I like your purpose. What you stand for is exciting, so I applied."

The answers to this question reveal their main motivation and the hot button that you're going to sell to throughout the recruiting process. Most candidates are smart enough to avoid bad-bucket answers, so if the candidate goes directly to salary and benefits, that's a sign that the person is selfish, and you probably don't want to go any further in the interview process with that person.

But if they're compelled to apply because of good reasons, that is a sign that the process should continue.

Second: "Why are you looking for a new position?"

With this question, you're trying to learn if leaving their current position to come work for you will solve a problem, or if it will just continue that problem.

For instance, if they say the main reason they're exploring your opportunity is, "I'm really tired of being on-call over the weekend," and you know your position requires weekend call hours, well, that's a mismatch. You might want to think twice about going further.

Or if they say, "I'm really tired of working for a doctor that micromanages me like crazy, I have to find something new," and you know that the doctor that you're hiring for has a reputation for micromanaging his Nurse Practitioners, then it's almost a nonstarter.

Attraction-based recruiting is describing a position in such a way that it touches on the most important motivators that drive people to seek a new job. Let's review those Five Prime Motivators for candidates again:

1. Work-life balance. More time with loved ones.

2. Ego. This position sounds prestigious. I would be proud to tell others what I do, and I am good at this.

3. Growth. The position offers a way to advance skills and improve career trajectory.

4. Proximity to loved ones. They want to be close to home.

5. Money. Typically people make a 5–10 percent increase in base salary when they take a new position. If they stay in their current job, on average people received a 2–3 percent increase each year.

DAVID WOLFE

When a candidate looks for a new position, their motivation will fall into one or more of those buckets. Your job is to find what the candidate's motivators are and sell to those. Are they looking at this position because it's close to family? Does it offer better work/life balance? That's what you're trying to figure out in that first interview—which bucket the candidate fits into.

It's perfectly appropriate to talk about money and benefits later in the process, before an offer or at the time of an offer. But if they're talking about money and benefits and what's in it for them on the first phone interview, then they're typically not a team player. They're not the kind of person you want to build a world-class team around, because they're already talking about what's in it for them.

After the initial phone interview, we send the candidate what we call a candidate information sheet (CIS) to fill out. It has five to seven questions that ask them what their base salary is, what their desired salary is, and other good information about what's motivating them. The sheet does two things. First, it unlocks some of the other things that they're looking for in the position, so that we can sell to those pain points or hot buttons throughout the recruiting process.

Secondly, it shows whether the candidate can write. In most positions, there's a decent amount of writing, and you want to know if this person can form sentences well and use good grammar. They need to have that skill, and this is an indicator of whether they do or not.

A key part to this interview is to put yourself in their shoes and ask yourself, "Do the reasons they are looking for a new job sound valid and legitimate? Do they have good reasons for looking?" What great recruiters can do is hear what's not being said. They can pick up on what the candidate is hiding by being perceptive to voice tones, pauses, hesitations, rote stories, and lack of authenticity. Trust your gut here.

If you feel they are sincere and you feel their reasons for looking are good, then one of the most powerful things you can do is articulate their problem better than they can. Then they will automatically assume that you and your group are the answer. Here's an example: Say the candidate says something like, "I am putting in lots of hours, more than they said when I first came on board. And it's way more on-call than they said it would be." You can say something like, "I can completely understand; you are feeling burned out and stretched thin. You are missing your son's soccer games, and when you are there you're completely exhausted and not really engaged. And you're probably not compensated for those extra hours you are putting in. We hear this a lot." Because you have articulated their problem better than they could, they feel listened to and cared for, and are more likely to trust you and your group.

If you can articulate their problem better than they can, they will automatically assume you have the solution to their problem.

STEP THREE: GROUP INTERVIEW

By now, you have narrowed the candidate pool further, and are down to the three-to-five really good ones. Here is how you start to separate the best from the rest.

I believe in group interviews. Have the candidates meet formally with at least two and preferably three other people in a group setting. The simple reason for that is that other interviewers will see things that you can't see. Your fellow interviewers have different minds and different personalities, and they're going to pick up on things you didn't pick up on. As a group, you will be able to look at a candidate from different angles, whereas if you do it by yourself you only get one angle.

Whoever those two or three people are, you must make sure that those are the same people that interview the next candidate and the next candidate. Then, after you've interviewed all the

As a group, you will be able to look at a candidate from different angles, whereas if you do it by yourself you only get one angle.

candidates, you can sit down and really compare notes on who the ideal person for the position was and who has exactly what you want.

What should you look for when you're looking to fill out your interview group? They could either be fellow workers in your HR department, or from executive leadership, or other A-players on your team, or all the above. If you're a small practice and you don't have an HR team, or you don't have an executive leadership team, then pick two of your top-performing A-players and have them sit in with you. They know what a team player and a high performer looks like, because they are one.

One trick I like is, at some point, after the candidate feels comfortable, you leave the room for a few minutes, so that the other two people can just talk to them and, hopefully, get the candidates to let their guard down a little bit. Then, come back in and ask them the following seven questions:

1. What metrics or numbers did you have to hit to know that you were winning in your role? (This can tell you whether they performed well and hit goals.)

2. Tell me about your proudest accomplishment and how you achieved it. (Was it something significant?)

3. Tell me about a failure. (Can they even admit they had one? Did they learn from it? How so?)

4. What did you like and dislike? (Does your position have the same things they disliked?)

5. How would you appraise your leader/supervisor? (Will their new leader in your position have these same characteristics?)

6. When we call, what will your boss say about your strengths and weaker points,

and how would your boss rate your overall performance, from one to five?

7. What are your reasons for leaving your current position? (Are they good reasons? Or is this candidate the real problem?)

With these seven questions, you're looking for patterns, for consistencies from position to position. For instance, does your candidate learn from mistakes or do failures repeat themselves in many jobs? During the interview, you're looking for how well they problem-solve, and if they learn from their mistakes. Also, how willing they are to admit their faults. That's a big one. How humble are they in that they admit that they were wrong? How much of a team player are they?

When you're asking all these questions, the true team player is a person who is really more about the team versus themselves. They're humble and coachable. They're driven. They're people-smart. That's really what you're looking for. You only want to hire people that have all three of these characteristics (more to come on this): (1) they're coachable, (2) they're driven, and (3) they're people-savvy.

I think one of the key questions is the last one: "How would your employer evaluate you, your strengths and weaknesses, and grade you on a scale of one to five?" I have found that the answer to that question will, 95 percent of the time, be the exact answer that you'll get from their reference—as long as they know that you are going to check the reference. That's why you want to preface it with, "I'm going to be checking references." They'll tell you because they know what the person's going to say.

The theory on this is, if you have the luxury of several candidates to choose from, you will only want the candidates that graded themselves and were graded by the employer a four or a five in all their previous positions. Ideally, if you go through their last four positions and they graded themselves a four or five and their boss or supervisor verified that, those are who you want. It's the people who are twos and threes who are typically lower performers.

After these three steps, it's time to dig a little deeper and learn more about the one or two candidates you think make the best match. The next three steps help you do that, with a standardized personal assessment, an unusual interview, and a closer look at the candidate at work.

Another great way to conduct an onsite interview, which we have only seen a few health systems do, is to have the candidate interview individually and separately with each member of the team. For example, they will have the NP interview and/or shadow with one MD for twenty to thirty minutes, then spend some time with the director of nursing, then the CEO, then a social worker. After the candidate meets with four to six people on the team, each team member fills out an evaluation card on the candidate completely separately from each other. This is done so each person forms their own unique opinion without outside influence. Then the team comes together and compares notes and decides on where the candidate is strongest and weakest.

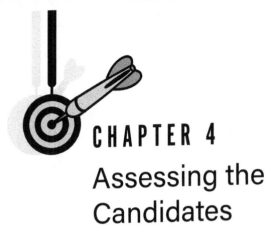

CHAPTER 4
Assessing the Candidates

"Organizational health trumps everything else in business."

—Patrick Lencion*i*

Let's face it: an interview is two people lying to each other. The hiring manager tells the candidate that everything is perfect and it is the greatest place to work in the world. The candidate says that she is nearly perfect in everything she does. Everybody gets into the interview mode and says what they think the other person wants to hear. It's all fake.

My nine-step process tries to cut through the interview mode and get behind the candidates' masks. The next three steps are specifically designed to do that.

The future workforce needs to be courted, not just interrogated. There needs to be a balance of appealing to their ego and vetting them. Old school methods of interrogation only won't work with this workforce. So be aware of this throughout the entire hiring process.

STEP FOUR: PERSONALITY ASSESSMENT

Most recruiters and hiring managers are familiar with personality assessments. They indicate how a person communicates, what type of personality they have, and how well—or poorly—they might fit within the team.

I particularly like the DiSC assessment. We have a resource that lets us give it to them for free. The test asks people to fill out a long questionnaire that tells a lot about their personality and behavior type. The personality assessment is really for communication purposes and how the direct supervisor or how people on the team are going to communicate with this new hire. For instance, if you want a really personable, outgoing Nurse Practitioner to help build up your urgent care practice, and you want that high-energy, entrepreneurial spirit, the DiSC test can identify that. You don't want the DiSC to show that the candidate is an introvert who is highly analytical and prefers to work alone for that position. It may be a disqualifier.

Or if you're hiring somebody who's going to work alone a lot and they're not going to interact with other staff members or see very many patients, you don't want to hire someone who is highly extroverted and who loves being around people. That might be a mismatch. It might be a non-starter. You might not want to go much further.

At the very least, it might trigger a conversation with the candidate. You get them on the phone and ask them questions about it. You need to be very blunt and frank with them: "Hey, here's some potential problems I see in this position. Your personality assessment indicates that you really like this, this, and this. But this position doesn't fit that. How do you feel you're going to respond in that position?" You can give them an opportunity to talk to you; maybe their explanation supersedes the DiSC profile and the potential mismatch. Or maybe they say, "You know what, I don't think I would be right for a position like that."

WHAT IS THE DISC ASSESSMENT?

According to the company's website (discprofile.com), the DiSC assessment helps those who take it increase self-knowledge about how you respond to conflict, what motivates you, what causes you stress, and how you solve problems. Knowing about a person's traits can help both the employee and employer improve working relationships by recognizing the communication needs of team members, facilitate better teamwork and teach productive conflict, develop stronger sales skills by identifying and responding to customer styles, and more effectively manage by understanding the dispositions and priorities of employees and team members.

The test breaks personalities into four categories, divided by the letters "DiSC":[13]

Dominance: A person whose score indicates they're a "D" type personality places emphasis on accomplishing results,

---

13   DISC, "What Is DiSC?" *DiSC*, www.discprofile.com/what-is-disc/overview/.

the bottom line, and confidence. Behaviors include:

- sees the big picture
- can be blunt
- accepts challenges
- gets straight to the point

Influence: A person whose score indicates they're a "I" type personality places emphasis on influencing or persuading others, openness, and relationships. Behaviors include:

- shows enthusiasm
- is optimistic
- likes to collaborate
- dislikes being ignored

Steadiness: A person whose score indicates they're a "S" type personality places emphasis on cooperation, sincerity, dependability. Behaviors include:

- doesn't like to be rushed
- calm manner
- calm approach
- supportive actions

Conscientiousness: A person whose score indicates they're a "C" type personality places emphasis on quality and accuracy, expertise, and competency. Behaviors include:

- enjoys independence
- objective reasoning
- wants the details
- fears being wrong

DiSC isn't the only assessment test out there. There's another one called Omnia®, which is designed specifically for hiring to fill a management position.[14] Omnia creates a benchmark profile for a management position supervising more than fifty people. The test shows how your candidate matches up against the ideal candidate. There are other tests out there, but those are the two main ones.

For me, the DiSC should be mandatory. Every hiring manager should require a DiSC profile on everybody that they're hiring. It not only helps with hiring, but we also use it in our daily communication with staff. We actually post our DiSC profile results on our desks in our office, which I recommend.

---

14 Omnia, https://www.omniagroup.com.

When we go to one person's desk we get familiar with their DiSC, and we know how to communicate with them. For instance, if I am a high C, I'm highly analytical and want tons of details about how things are done. If I go and talk to somebody who's a low C but a high D, I know I can't talk to him for thirty minutes about all the details on how things are going to be done. I've got to hit him with bullet points and give him the icing on the cake. If a high C goes into thirty minutes of detail with somebody who's a high D, then you're going to lose them. They might even lose respect for you because that is not how they communicate. You have to tailor your communication toward that person's DiSC assessment.

Here's another example. The "I" type is Influential. That person is extroverted. They like a high number of contacts. They want to have fun. A high "C," who's very fact based and detailed, has to communicate with an "I" differently. They may need to shoot the breeze with them for a while and talk about their weekend. An "I" wants to do a lot of rapport building before they get into the details.

An "S" is somebody who's really steady. They want everything to stay the same. They don't want things to change. They want a steady pace. They may find conflict with a "D," who can be impulsive, likes to change course, and moves quickly.

Not only does this help in choosing who you hire, but it can also give insight into *how* you hire. When an "S" is hiring, for instance, they may lean toward hiring somebody who doesn't rock the boat. When a "C" is hiring, they may prefer hiring a conscientious person for the position. When a "D" is hiring, they may want to hire really fast and, as a result, make a decision based on the first two people they interview. An "I" wants to make sure that they hire someone who gets along with everybody socially and has fun. So it's a good idea for the hiring manager to take the DiSC test to understand how their own personality affects and colors their hiring behaviors.

STEP FIVE: CONDUCT AN UNUSUAL INTERVIEW

As I said earlier, an interview is just two people lying to each other. The goal throughout the whole interview process is to remove those interview masks. Nothing does it better than holding

An interview is just two people lying to each other.

an interview outside the normal context of over the phone or in the office.

This step helps get rid of the interview masks so that you can see the real person. Some people are phenomenal during the face-to-face interview and the phone interview. They're masters at it. Maybe they're super con artists or they're really good communicators, or they think on their feet very well. You don't want to evaluate them solely based on how well they talk in the first phone call and the face-to-face interview. Some people are really gifted at it and they'll fool you. This step can really remove the interview mask and let you know whether the person is a true team player—if they're coachable, driven, and people-savvy.

Take the candidate out. Have people on your team take the candidate out for lunch or dinner or for drinks. Preface it to the candidate as, "Hey, I want you to get to know our team, get to know our company culture, and to get a feel for whether you think we would be a good fit for you, as much as it is we're trying to get a good feel for you." Every organization has their own version of crazy, so you're asking the candidate, "Do you want to be around our version of crazy? It's a way for you to evaluate us."

When they get outside the office, the team can ask them questions, shoot the breeze, and really get to know them. They are actually evaluating them and how they interact with other people. That's the key indicator. Are they a jerk? Are they self-centered? You're trying to get at that by getting them to let their guard down. Notice how they interact with the server. Do they treat the server like they're a servant, or do they treat the server with the same respect as anybody else? How do they interact with the person on your team who might seem to have the lowest rank? Do they treat that person with the same level of integrity and kindness that they treat the boss or the person who is hiring them? Sometimes, when candidates let their guard down, they'll say stuff off the cuff that will give your team an indicator of who this person really is. This is a really valuable step.

In some cases, when working with hospitals, we've seen employers ask realtors to give prospects a tour of the community if the candidate would have to relocate from out of town. The realtor will schedule a half day with the person and, in the course of the half day, learn a lot. The candidate will reveal all kinds of things about themselves and their motives, and that might turn up a really big red flag.

For instance, they could say something like, "I'm not really interested in this job. I just wanted a free trip to Chicago to see my sister. I'm going on this tour with you because they want me to do the tour." Or the candidate may treat the realtor as beneath them or act cocky and abrasive. That's not the type of person that you want to hire. They're not humble and they're not coachable. They don't have the traits that make a team player.

Another possibility: run errands together. I've heard of people trying this. The recruiter says, "I've got to go pick up my kids from soccer practice. I've got a time crunch. Do you mind if we go in the car and talk there?" You might get to see how they interact with kids. You're trying to pick up on some cues.

This step is not a common practice, but more and more hiring groups are doing it. It's becoming more and more utilized because people are seeing the value in it. Many hiring managers have said, "If I would have done this step, I would have saved myself so much of a headache, because I would have realized this person was toxic and I would have never let him in the building." It's highly under-utilized, and it might be tricky to try to figure out how you're going to do it. But come up with a way that you can sneak it in, especially for a higher-level position that is going to be interacting with a lot of patients, a lot of team members, and be a face for your organization. You don't want to skip this step.

STEP SIX: ASK THE CANDIDATE TO PERFORM ACTUAL WORK FOR YOU

What's the best way to see how someone will fit in with your company? Get them to do some work for you. Get a feel for the level of their work ethic, and also get a feel for who they really are and if they are really a team player. This is definitely an optional step, but highly recommended.

For example, ask a Nurse Practitioner candidate to shadow another Nurse Practitioner for four hours, or two hours, or a full day, whatever you can arrange. Present it as a chance for the candidate to ask that Nurse Practitioner working questions. That Nurse Practitioner on your team can report back what they're hearing and what type of questions they're asking. They might be asking red flag questions or talking about things that set off alarms.

Or, let's say you're hiring a human resource assistant. Maybe you can get them to come in for four hours to do some administrative tasks. That could give you a feel for this person's work ethic. Were they hungry enough and driven enough to come into work for four hours, potentially for free? If that person is willing to come for two to four hours and actually do some work unpaid, that shows you how motivated they are and how much they want the position. And during that four-hour period, you're evaluating the quality and the hustle in their work.

You want to get with your person afterward and try to get a feel for whether the candidate was coachable, driven, and people-savvy. Did the candidate seem like they really knew their stuff clinically and professionally? This is a little bit of an extension of the previous step of the outside interview. It's just another indicator.

It doesn't have to be free work. Some groups pay candidates in a gift card to a local restaurant or simply a Visa gift card to reimburse them for some work that they did.

As I said, this step is optional. But I recommended it, and a lot of the groups we work with do it. They like it, and find it is worth doing. You often see something pop up that's valuable, that prevents you from hiring somebody crazy and toxic. You don't want to let the wrong person in the building so that you're losing patients and your current staff is stressed out and doesn't want to work with this person.

After you've conducted these six steps, you should know if one or two of the candidates are a good match. Before you make an offer, though, there are three more steps to take to make sure you have attracted the A-player you need. Let's take a look at those in the next chapter.

CHAPTER 5
Making the Offer

You've sent dozens of candidates through the first six steps of the funnel, and now one or two have made it through. But you're not done yet. There are three more steps to follow before you have the perfect candidate hired. If you don't, you could end up with a story like the following.

Earlier this year, we did a rural primary care NP search in West Virginia. The position was open for three months before we started the search. We sent them three matching candidates within two weeks, and they loved one of them. From the beginning, we were clear with the hiring manager the candidate needed $105,000 in salary in order to accept the position. It was in writing and was mentioned numerous times. They went through the hiring process very fast and followed only three steps. When it came down to making the offer, the hiring manager did it verbally over the phone and offered $95,000 in hopes of negotiating and meeting in the middle and saving a little money. Of course, the NP was shocked, because she was clear what her salary expectations were. The NP stopped communicating with the hiring manager and turned down the offer. She wanted this position more than other positions, but the others offered her more. She also didn't feel valued or heard, so she thought this wasn't a good long-term fit for her.

This type of scenario happens often and leads to lots of wasted time, and worse: not getting the A-players. In the next three steps, I will go over how to conclude the recruitment process and help ensure you close the deal and land A-players.

STEP SEVEN: REFERENCE CHECKS

I've heard it said before that a reference check is a "stupid" check. If somebody's stupid enough to pick a bad reference, they are too stupid to hire. Most references, we know, are typically going to say good things about the person. That makes reference checks tricky; you know the candidate is only going to pick references who will say glowing things about them. That's why I do things a bit differently here, in order to ensure that I get valuable information.

Have the Candidate Set Up the Reference Calls for You.

Ask the candidate to actually set up the reference call with a direct supervisor or a direct report. You want them to schedule the time and tell you who to call and when. This forces them to take the initiative. It shows you that they really want

A-players cant wait for you to hear how their previous supervisors rate them.

this job, to the point that they have set up interviews for you.

Also, A-players tend to be excited about reference checks—they can't wait for their boss or supervisor to talk directly to you. On the other hand, sometimes lower performers really don't want that. Those C-players can't seem to get hold of the references, or they can't seem to find supervisory references and give you a lot of peer references, which can be a big red flag.

Ask the candidate to find and schedule at least two direct supervisory references. A third or fourth reference can be a peer, but you want to talk to supervisors.

Ask Questions in a Different Way.

If you dig a little, you can address areas of concern
you had during the interview. If there are a couple
of things you aren't sure about in the candidate, ask
probing questions and address your exact concerns to
the reference, and allow the reference to speak about
it openly. For example, two years ago I was doing a
reference check for an internal hire I was about to
make. In order to put the reference at ease (and get
insightful information), I explained that I was calling
to see if he thought this person would fit this specific
role well, and whether she would fit our company
culture. I explained that I wasn't calling just to see
if this employee was a good employee; there is an
important distinction here. I explained the type of
role this was and the type of company we were.

When I asked the reference to discuss the candidate's weaknesses, he said, "None that I can think of,"
which is what most people say at first. Then I rephrased
it and said, "Obviously no employee is perfect. If
there were one or two things you think she needs to
improve on most, what would they be?" There was a
pause; I waited in the awkward silence. Finally, reluc-
tantly, he started to speak about that. I then began
to ask him some clarifying questions, and he slowly
started to open up. I ended up getting some great

information that didn't prevent me from hiring the person but gave me critical insight on how I would coach and develop this person in the future.

When references are reluctant to say anything negative, you have to dig. No one's perfect, everyone has weak spots. What's the candidate's Achilles heel? What was the thing that you most got frustrated with? What was the thing that the candidate didn't do so well? Keep digging until you get something to work with.

Asking questions this way gives the reference an out. They aren't saying anything bad about this person, just talking about what they need to improve on. Your big objective is to figure out what the candidate's weaknesses are and what they struggle with. That's why we preface that question by saying no employee is perfect. It gives the reference a way to talk freely about the person without being overtly negative.

Ask the Reference the Same Question You Asked the Candidate.

Another key to reference checks is to ask the reference the same question that you asked the candidate during the interview. Remember that you asked the candidate how their supervisor would assess the person's strengths and weaknesses and how they would rank them on a scale from one to five. Now you can see how well the supervisor aligns with how they answered that question during the interview. Most of the time it'll be pretty well matched—and it should match. If there's a discrepancy, that might show how self-aware and people-savvy the candidate is.

Check the References the Candidate Didn't Give You.

One very powerful technique is to check the references that aren't on their list. For instance, if they didn't include a supervisory reference from an earlier employer, and you happen to know who works there or you can find out easily who works there, you can just spot-check that reference. Go do some digging on your own and call around. This extra reference can often give you information you need to know—information that maybe the candidate didn't want you to know—which can save you from hiring a bad apple.

One very powerful technique is to check the references that aren't on their list.

STEP EIGHT: BACKGROUND CHECKS

This is pretty standard. When we recruit for hospitals, they have their background checks and drug screens all set up and squared away already.

If you're a smaller company and you don't typically do background checks, I encourage you to do so. It isn't hard to find companies that perform background checks—a Google search is one avenue and asking people you know in HR positions at bigger firms for recommendations is another. Lab companies like LabCorps and Quest Diagnostics do drug screening tests.

These final tests are important. You don't want to learn the kind of information that comes from these tests too late. If you are new to this, when you make an offer to a candidate you can stipulate that the offer is contingent on these background checks. Keep yourself covered in case anything damaging surfaces.

STEP NINE: MAKE THE OFFER

Everything checks out. The references answered your questions to your satisfaction, and the background check raised no red flags. You have the best candidate available. You are almost ready to make the offer.

First, though, take a deep breath and review the following characteristics that indicate the candidate has the perfect blend of attributes that you need in each hire in order to build a world-class team. If not, follow up with more questions.

The Three Virtues You Need in Everyone You Hire: Driven, Coachable, and People-Savvy.

IS THE CANDIDATE DRIVEN?

If you aren't 100 percent sold that this candidate is driven, here are some questions that you can ask to give you more insight.

- "What's the one thing in your life you put the most effort into achieving?" You are checking to see if they have ever really applied themselves.

- "Give me an example of something you succeeded in." You are looking for a history of success in anything; if they have really put themselves out there and tried something and had some success, that shows the type of drive a person has. On my team I have a former NCAA gymnast, a professional baseball player from the Arizona Diamondbacks, and an Army Ranger with multiple Purple Hearts. It doesn't have to be a work-related success, as you can see, just something that shows they have the drive to put their mind to the task at hand.

- "What do you enjoy doing outside of work?" If someone has a huge list of all the things they love to do, then there is a chance that you and your new position will never compete with all their activities and interests.

- "What is your greatest accomplishment in life?" Check to see how hard it was to achieve and what adversity they had to face.

IS THE CANDIDATE COACHABLE?

As a college baseball coach, I saw that freshman often have a hard time making adjustments to college-level pitching and hitting. They

Everyone needs to be coachable and moldable if they want to get better. You only want to hire coachable people that want to learn and grow.

think that what worked for them in high school will work for them in college, which isn't true. The same is true in any profession. Everyone needs to be coachable and moldable if they want to get better. You only want to hire coachable people that want to learn and grow.

If you aren't 100 percent sold that this candidate is coachable, here are some questions that you can ask to give you more insight.

- "Describe to me your best teacher or coach and tell me how they helped you." Do they admit they sought and received help? Or is all their success due to their own efforts?

- "Tell me about an important accomplishment in your life." Do they only use the word "I" or do they use "we" also? If they only use "I," this could be an indicator the person is uncoachable and not humble.

- "How have you most changed over the past five years?" Have they changed, and can they admit their weaknesses? Or do they claim to have always had it all together?

- "What is one area of your life that you are working to improve currently?" Does the person even think they need to work on anything?

IS THE CANDIDATE PEOPLE-SAVVY?

If you aren't 100 percent sold that this candidate is people-savvy, here are ways to get more insight.

The best indicator of this is when you took them out socially or got them outside of the normal interview mode. How did they treat the waitress? Realtor? Administrative assistant? Do they treat everyone the same, or do they show preferential treatment depending on whom they deem important?

You can also ask:

- "Describe to me your personality." How aware of themselves are they? Does it match with what you or your team see and what their DiSC profile reveals? If it's off, or if they are stumped by this question, that is not a good sign.

- "Can you describe to me a time where you displayed compassion toward a teammate?" Do they even describe compassion well? Do they value it?

- If you want to build a world-class team that's really going to do some awesome things, you don't want to let anybody in your doors that does not have all three of these characteristics. When you are convinced this candidate does, make an offer.

Put the Offer in Writing.

An offer letter is powerful. It is okay to say to them, "We're going to make an offer, but I'm going to email it to you so you can see it in writing." I like the psychology of them seeing the offer in writing. Before sending the offer, verbally tell them exactly why you chose them. Be specific about all the people you evaluated, and then be specific about why you chose them. What are the attributes that you liked about them that made you pick them? That gets the relationship off to a great start, because you are complimenting them and it shows that you put a lot of thought into this.

For instance, if I'm hiring a recruiter for our office, when I make the offer I might say, "Close to two hundred people showed interest in this position. I interviewed thirteen people over the phone, and I brought four people in for face-to-face interviews, and you were our number-one choice. We saw that you have all the attributes to be successful at NP Now. We think that based on all your previous accomplishments and personality, you would fit very well into this new role." Whatever the reasons are, be specific on why you chose them. That gets them excited to join your team.

I know that with some positions there aren't many good candidates, such as hiring an NP, for example. In some locations there may only be one candidate to consider, and you may be forced to hire a less-than-perfect fit just to keep your clinic open. This happens often when we recruit NPs and PAs into rural areas. But you still want that person to feel like they got into Harvard or MIT. You still want to drive them through the process and make them feel that this is a special place to work, and you don't hire just anybody. You only hire first-rate people—A-players.

Another benefit of putting the offer in writing is this: I have found that candidates are less likely to negotiate if they see the offer in a formal letter with your company logo on it. When you make the offer verbally, you might sense some initial disappointment, some hesitancy because the number offered doesn't match what they had in mind. That can set you up for potentially getting the relationship off to a bad start.

Make Your Best Offer First.

If your best offer is $100,000, make it. We see hiring managers make the mistake of offering less and trying to negotiate. Many people, especially millennials, are leaving jobs because they don't feel valued and appreciated. So if the first impression they get from you is that you're low-balling them, it resonates with them and can also say to them, "We do not value and appreciate you." I recommend making your best offer first versus trying to negotiate back and forth. It says you value them and want them. And even if you do overpay somebody by a little bit, that's going to pay dividends in the end with retention.

In fact, I believe it's always better to pay more for every position you're recruiting for. Pay 10 percent to 20 percent more than the market value. That person will feel like you really want them, and you don't have to worry as much about them being picked off for a higher-paying job later. It's not really a win if you pay someone less, because they are more likely to leave you for a higher-paying position later. You also don't have to be as concerned about giving raises. If you already started them off high, they might not be expecting raises every single year.

Paying a little bit more creates a sense of trust between employee and employer. And it gets the relationship off on a good foot. There's going to be enough things that could go wrong during their employment, it's so important to start it on the right foot by making a good and generous offer versus trying to low ball and negotiate.

Include Bonus Compensation.

Most of our hospital systems really miss out on go-getter A-players because they don't let them know about their bonus system. That's a big selling point to somebody who is really driven. You need to advertise that upfront, in the job description and the final offer.

Be specific. "You can earn $20,000 to $40,000 a year depending on productivity benchmarks." That can be a really big selling point.

Be Prepared to Walk Away.

Even with a high offer and a generous bonus package, your candidate may want more. If you have truly made your best offer—as I recommend—explain that you are already above market rate, and you can go no higher. Be honest about it. But then, be prepared to let the candidate go.

The truth is, when you follow these nine steps, and you have brought up salary expectations throughout the entire three- to five-week hiring process, that will almost never happen. By then, you have found a candidate who has the three characteristics of success, who finds value in other things than money, and who fits your company culture and wants to work for you. That's the power of attraction-based recruiting.

And now comes the next important phase of your relationship: retaining your A-players in the millennial age.

Example of a 4 Week Hiring Timeline

OCT 1	OCT 3	OCT 6	OCT 18	OCT 18 – OCT 31	NOV 1

OCT 1 Resume received

OCT 3 Contact them within 72 hours

OCT 6 Phone interview scheduled by October 6

OCT 18 Site visit by October 18

OCT 18 – OCT 31 Get to know them outside of an interview environment
Have them take a personality test
Have them shadow at your location for a few hours
Do a reference check
Get a background check

NOV 1 Make an offer by November 1

If you need help understanding or establishing any of these, or for more information, come to me.

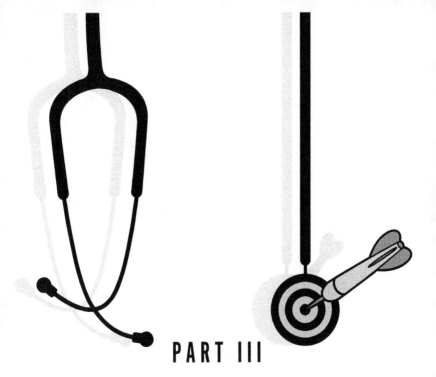

PART III

RETAINING "THE FUTURE WORKFORCE"

CHAPTER 6

Understanding the Future Workforce

Millennials now make up the biggest portion of the workforce. By 2025, 75 percent of all workers will be millennials.[15] For those who will be recruiting, hiring, and retaining these workers, it is critically important to get inside their heads and understand who they are, what their values are, and what value they can bring to your organization. That's the only way to know that you're hitting on these while recruiting them and, perhaps as important, to retain them long term.

First, some definitions are in order. How old are the millennials? That depends on who you ask. The dates range from birthdates from the late 1970s to the early 2000s, but most demographers place those born between about 1980 and about 2000 in the millennial generation. So today, in 2018, millennials

---

15 Debra Donston-Miller, "Workforce 2020: What You Need to Know."

are those workers between the ages of about eighteen and thirty-eight, give or take.

I am at the cusp of that generation. I think that helps me understand their thinking, while also putting me at the older end, so I have the perspective and some of the traits of the previous generation. I think I have a handle on what makes them tick. On top of that, the majority of the staff on my team at NP Now are aged twenty-six to thirty-two. I have done a lot of research to try to figure out what's really going on with this age group.

Let's talk about the preconceptions first.

They Have a Bad Reputation.

When you hear the term *millennial*, what comes to mind? Unless you are in that generation yourself, it's probably not good. A lot of negative things are being said about this generation—more than positive things. But when you think about it, most generations start off with a bad reputation. The younger generation rarely delights the older generations.

I don't think this is anything new. The post-World War II generation complained about the baby boomers. Then the baby boomers complained about Gen X workers. It's human nature to think you know more than those who come after you, that your way is the best way, and that "these kids" are just that: kids.

Like all generations, millennials have traits that can be both good and bad in the work environment. Millennials are considered entitled, selfish, and impatient. They are called lazy and disloyal. They need a lot of hand holding. They're still under the influence of Mom and Dad.

There is probably some level of truth to all of those conceptions, or else people wouldn't say them. But my argument is there's some level of truth to those traits for *every* generation when they are in their twenties to early thirties. There may have been slightly different aspects of what their weaker points were and what their stronger points were, but the baby boomers, the Gen Xers, and all the other generations were in some way immature and self-centered at that age.

Millennials are singled out for being especially entitled. I could probably go on for hours about why—the "everybody gets a trophy" mentality they were raised with, etc. But I don't want to go into the reasons they may be entitled or impatient or less loyal. I want to focus on their strengths and how to use those when hiring and retaining them as workers. It requires cracking their code and adjusting, figuring out how to motivate and engage and recruit this workforce, versus sitting on your hands and complaining. A lot of hiring managers may be toward the end of their career and are complaining about this generation rather than doing something about it. They're just hurting their organization by complaining about it, instead of stepping up and doing something.

They Are Tech-Savvy.

We need to understand this generation is technology-centered. They grew up in a fast-paced culture. They're tech-savvy. They're creative. They think outside of the box, and they know how to find answers and resources quickly. They've been exposed to more technology than previous generations were. They live in this constant flow of idea-sharing on the Internet and through social media. They grew up in the world of constant feedback, so they have a lot of information they can access in an instant.

We need to understand this generation is technology-centered.

I think they have information overload, but that also gives them a framework to use to your company's advantage. Because they have all this information and have been exposed to all these things, they are uniquely able to think about a problem in a new way to give your business fresh ideas. If they have a voice in the company to share their ideas and suggest how things can be done better, employers might find they do have great ideas and opinions about how things could be done.

They Are Diverse.

According to a report published by the Brookings Institute, American millennials are by far the most diverse generation in our history.[16] Most of the baby boomers and their parents and grandparents were born when immigration was historically low, and the immigrants who did come to America were mostly white Europeans, the institute says. The nation's minority population was much smaller than it is now and was predominately African American in highly segregated cities. However, large numbers of immi-

---

16   William H. Frey, "The Millennial Generation: A Demographic Bridge to America's Future," *Brookings Institute*, January 2018, www.brookings.edu/research/millennials.

grants to the US in the 1980s and 1990s, especially from Latin America and Asia, along with an aging white population, "has made millennials a more racially and ethnically diverse generation than any that preceded it," the report concludes.

They Want to Succeed.

A big facet of this trait is learning what their strengths are and letting them be free to use them to help you. This can greatly help grow your company and your organization, while it gives them exactly what they need. The biggest desire millennials want out of work is to feel like they're really good at what they're doing. They want to be great at it; they want to be an expert at it. That's a big positive attribute and capitalizing on that and getting them the tools they need so that they can be really good at their job is a key strategy for hiring and retaining them.

They Can Multitask.

They typically do well in jobs that require multitasking and switching from one project to the next. They are adept at keeping multiple, concurrent projects going at the same time. In fact, that drives them. They also tend to like collaborating. They're really good at sharing ideas without getting their feelings hurt. I think they're a little bit better than some other generations. They're a little bit more open to kicking things around and talking, as opposed to taking orders from above. I believe they are a little bit more abstract in their thinking, not as black and white, which can also help an organization thrive and adapt in a swiftly changing marketplace.

Whatever You Do—Don't Call Them Millennials!

The millennial label hasn't been a positive one. They have been called selfish, entitled, lazy job-hoppers. They know that, so when they hear that label, I think it makes them clam up. It doesn't create a positive emotion in them. It doesn't sit well with them. From here on, let's call them the future workforce.

The fact of the matter is, whatever you call them and whatever their strengths and weaknesses may be, that doesn't negate the fact that this is the future workforce. We have to learn how to attract them. And we want to only hire the best of this future workforce, and then retain the best of this workforce.

Adjust or Lose

You have no choice; this is the workforce for the foreseeable future. And they are coming fast, especially in healthcare. A lot of providers are aging out. The average physician is in their early fifties.[17] The average age of a Nurse Practitioner is forty-nine years old.[18] By 2030, AAMC projects a physician shortage of one hundred thousand MDs.[19] Many will be retiring in the next five to ten years. They're going to be replaced by this generation.

So what you'll learn in the next chapter are the four ways to retain these workers. I suggest you start developing these strategies now, instead of sitting on your hands and complaining or waiting till you retire in ten years and letting it be someone else's problem. Put these ideas in place now, so you can make your organization better now, and you can leave your organization better than when you came in. Make

---

17 "Distribution of U.S. physicians by age group in 2016," Statista, https://www.statista.com/statistics/415961/share-of-age-among-us-physicians.

18 "NP Fact Sheet," American Association of Nurse Practitioners, last modified August 20, 2018, https://www.statista.com/statistics/415961/share-of-age-among-us-physicians.

19 Atul Grover, "New 2025 Physician Workforce Projections," Association of American Medical Colleges, March 25, 2015, https://www.aamc.org/download/428616/data/20150401_projbriefingppt.pdf.

an adjustment now because things change faster and move faster. It's much harder to play catch up.

I have heard it said that recruiters feel like they need to lower their standards for this future workforce. That's not the case at all. Keep the standards the same or make them even higher. You will still get the right people on your team. Make the adjustments that follow and try to get them in place as soon as possible. Learn what the hot buttons are in this workforce so you can attract and recruit them. You will give yourself a better chance at building a really good team and, in the process, give your organization a competitive advantage.

"THE NEW FACE OF AMERICA"

"Millennials of all racial and ethnic backgrounds can make the case that investing in a more inclusive America is essential to the nation's economic success and will, as well, benefit older populations. As they move into middle age, millennials will represent the new face of America in business, in politics, in popular culture, and as the nation's image to the rest of the world."[20]

20 Frey, "Millennials."

Six Interesting Facts About Millennials

1. An estimated 8 percent of new graduates brought their parents to an interview according to an Adecco survey cited in the *Wall Street Journal* (*WSJ*). What's more, a full 3 percent actually had their parents sit in on their job tryout.[21]

2. More than two thousand parents joined their children at Google's second "Take Your Parents to Work" day at its Mountain View, California, headquarters, the *WSJ* reported.[22]

3. In 2007, the Collegiate Employment Research Institute at Michigan State University published a survey of 725 employees and found that nearly 25 percent of employers encountered parental involvement during the hiring process and the early stages of their children's working careers. Within that group of employers,

21 *Anita Hofschneider*, "Should You Bring Mom and Dad to the Office?" *Wall Street Journal*, September 10, 2013, https://www.wsj.com/articles/hiring-millennials-meet-the-parents-1378856472?KEYWORDS=millennial&tesl a=y.

22 Ibid.

more than 30 percent reported parents submitting a resume for their children, 15 percent reported fielding complaints from a parent when the company didn't hire their child, and nearly 10 percent said parents had inserted themselves into salary and benefit negotiations.[23]

4. A LinkedIn survey on people who had changed jobs found that 59 percent of respondents chose their new company because they saw a stronger career path or more opportunity there—not because of money.[24]

5. A 2015 LinkedIn survey found that 36 percent of respondents changed jobs because they were unsatisfied with the work environment or culture—not because of money.[25]

---

23 Phil Gardner, "Parent Involvement in the College Recruiting Process: To What Extent?" Collegiate Employment Research Institute at Michigan State University, 2007, http://ceri.msu. edu/publications/pdf/ceri2-07.pdf.

24 Ester Cruz, "New LinkedIn Report Reveals the Latest Job Seeking Trends," LinkedIn Talent Blog, June 27, 2016, https://business.linkedin.com/ talent-solutions/blog/trends-and-research/2016/ linkedin-new-report-reveals-the-latest-job-seeking-trends.

25 Kaytie Zimmerman, "Millennials, Stop Apologizing for Job-Hopping," *Forbes* online, June 7, 2016, https://

6. The PEW Research Center found that younger millennials stay in jobs an average of thirteen months—which is the same as Gen Xers when they were in their twenties.[26]

Millennials' Job Tenure No Shorter than that of Prior Generation

% of 18- to 35-year-old workers by length of employment with current employer

13 months or more

Millennial in 2016	63.4%
Gen X in 2000	59.9

5 years or more

Millennial in 2016	22.0
Gen X in 2000	21.8

Note: Workers refers to wage and salary workers. The self-employed are not included.

Note: Workers refers to wage and salary workers. The self-employed are not included. Workers who have worked for their current emlpoyer for more than one year are considered to have worked 13 months or more. Workers who have worked for their current employer for more than four years are considered to have worked five years or more. Gen X in 2000 includes workers born between 1965 and 1982 and includes some older Millennials born after 1980.

Source: Pew Research Center analysis of Current Population Survey Displaced Worker Supplements.

---

www.forbes.com/sites/kaytiezimmerman/2016/06/07/millennials-stop-apologizing-for-job-hopping/#18f1ac374656.

26 Richard Fry, "Millenials aren't job-hopping any faster than Generation X did," Fact Tank, April 19, 2017, http://www.pewresearch.org/fact-tank/2017/04/19/millennials-arent-job-hopping-any-faster-than-generation-x-did.

CHAPTER 7

The Four Best Ways to Grow and Retain the Future Workforce

"Nobody cares how much you know, until they know how much you care."

—Theodore Roosevelt

NP Now became the number-one Nurse Practitioner search firm in 2016, and has grown 30 to 50 percent almost every year, with a staff made up mostly of this future workforce. Here in Charleston, South Carolina, where we're located, we can pick the best people and let only the best into our company culture and our organization. We don't just talk the talk. We walk the walk. We have a staff full of A-players. And most importantly, we keep them.

We have had 92 percent retention and not one person has ever voluntarily left the company. That's says a lot because we require a lot from everyone on the team. Retention is vital, as any organization knows. With the cost of a vacant position so high, and the cost of recruiting a new hire so high, nothing saves more money than keeping a high-performing team member in place.

That's not easy with this generation of so-called selfish and entitled workers. I hope I set that record straight in the previous chapter. The fact is, within any generation, there are people who are coachable, driven, and people-savvy. Those are the ones you want to hire, and the nine steps I have outlined in the previous chapters will help you find them.

Keeping them is the next phase. For that, I have developed four ways to grow and retain these employees. I've come up with this process after a lot of research, testing, and working with a consulting firm that specifically builds younger teams and applying it in my business.

Having a consistent person in front of clients is so important in my business—and that translates to Nurse Practitioners and other health providers. RNs and NPs change jobs every 2.6 years, so retention can be a game-changer. If you can crack the code on this younger workforce, and get them to stay with you five, seven, or ten years, think about the competitive advantage that gives you.

That's the mentality behind the approach I've taken in creating these four steps to grow and retain the new workforce.

1. STRESS YOUR PURPOSE.

Everybody wants to feel like they're part of something bigger than them, and that they're contributing to something bigger than them. I think this future workforce really wants a job that hits this sweet spot. It's a really big passion for them, so living this is very important.

Your core purpose is why you do what you do.

The first part of creating a bigger purpose is creating a winning organization. People naturally want to join organizations that are winning. If the perception and the reality is that you are doing really cool things and winning, people are naturally attracted to that. As stated earlier in the book, I learned this while I coached college baseball at San Francisco State and Charleston Southern University. No matter how hard I tried to recruit kids to these programs—come join our team, make an immediate impact, be a starting player from day one, be a star—nine times out of ten, they would choose the bigger school, the Pac-12 school, or the SEC school because they wanted to be a part of the image of a bigger school and a well-known team, even though they might sit at the bench and not play for two or three years.

What that means for you is figuring out how you're winning and selling that, both in recruiting and in retaining the team members you have hired. How are you winning? How are you doing big things? Even if it's something really small, make sure it is prominent. What are you doing in the community that's different than other medical practices? Whether it's the number of patients you're serving in the county, or your patient satisfaction scores, or the tenure you have within your team, whatever it is, you want to pull that out and sell it to your staff constantly. Keep them immersed in a feeling of winning.

I think the second facet of this is having that strong core purpose, core values, and vision. This younger workforce is really sensitive to the ideas that support the cool things you do and why you're doing what you do. As I have said, our core purpose is, "We connect people to improve lives." We're improving our hiring managers' lives and making their lives easier by finding them top-notch NPs. We're increasing revenue for the practice. And we're improving NPs' lives by finding better jobs for them and their family, and perhaps they are earning more money.

Disney's core purpose is, "We make people happy." Walmart's core purpose is, "We save people money so they can live better." What is your core purpose? If your organization doesn't have a clear core purpose, create one and then make it real.

Next, present a vision of where your company is going. What exactly do you want to accomplish in the next ten years? This needs to be big enough that people want to get behind it. Jim Collins calls it a BHAG—Big Hairy Audacious Goal. Our ten-year vision is to place six hundred NPs and PAs in 2027 and improve the lives of that many NPs and medical centers. Creating some sort of clear vision for your company is really important. This is not a mission statement or a core value. This is something that has metrics that you can measure to know whether you're hitting it. This younger population, they're looking for where you are going and what you are trying to accomplish.

Another part of creating your bigger purpose, and one that this younger workforce is really attracted to, is contributing to charity. Maybe you give 1 percent of all your sales to a certain charity, or a certain percentage of profit goes toward helping developing areas without food or clean water, or maybe it's disaster relief, or diaper giveaways. Whatever it is, it can and should be a big selling point to your current staff. They want to know that every day they come to work, their company is affecting other people's lives in a big way. They will definitely get behind that.

We are not alone in this. Companies are upping their community service and donations like crazy, and I think part of the reason for that is because this younger workforce is responding to it. By the way, some customers actually choose the companies they do business with because of that as well. A lot of those customers are the younger generation.

To sum this point up, the younger workforce wants to feel a part of something bigger, and that they are having an impact in that big picture. They want to be part of a winning organization. In the recruitment process, it's important to hit on

The younger workforce wants to feel a part of something bigger, and that they are having an impact in that big picture.

all these things, but then when they come on board, you have to actually do these things. It's not a bait and switch—you are delivering, and they can feel it within the company culture. Most of these things that I've just mentioned are not costly, they're not a financial drain. They're simple. If you don't have them, use your team to create them, which creates more power. If this workforce can create the vision and core purpose and take part in the great things you do, then they're going to buy in more. And when your organization's on fire, your retention numbers will skyrocket.

2. FOSTER MENTORSHIP AND LEADERSHIP.

I think that this future workforce really craves solid leadership. They want to be managed early in their career. They want to have to live up to a high standard. So mentorship and leadership are critically important. Mentorship and leadership can be two separate things. A worker should have a mentor, which I recommend, someone they look up to and want to emulate. Leadership can come from that same person, but the leadership piece is more about somebody who will hold the team accountable and cast a vision for the team member. Maybe that person is their direct report, a supervisor who sets the clear expectations and then holds them accountable.

I think some of this has been lost over the past ten years. It's become kind of uncool to hold people accountable in the "everyone gets a trophy" era. But I've found that people on your team thrive on that accountability. It helps them stay focused. The number-one thing that this generation of workers is looking for is to do something that they can excel at.

To guide them, you must be very clear on your expectations and show them what winning looks like. Yet, according to a Gallup poll, 49 percent of all employees across all organizations do not know exactly what is expected of them.[27] So if you asked about half of your workforce what their key metrics are, they wouldn't know. How can they know what winning looks like in that scenario? They can't. So, step one is holding them accountable by setting some clear expectations. These can be called Key Result Areas (KRAs) or Key Performance Indicators (KPIs). They include metrics and numbers, and it's usually

---

27   Marco Nink, "Many Employees Don't Know What's Expected of Them at Work," Gallup, October 13, 2015, https://news.gallup.com/businessjournal/186164/employees-don-know-expected-work.aspx.

just two or three numbers, that can tell them whether they're winning or not.

For a Nurse Practitioner, it could be a KPI of seeing a minimum of fifteen patients per day over the course of a month, and an expectation of patient satisfaction scores to be above a certain percentage and setting up a certain number of follow-up appointments. There are three different metrics that they can see on paper, and if they hit those three numbers, then they know they're winning.

Then it takes a good leader to hold them accountable. We've found that following up with metrics weekly is the best way to do it. Waiting every month lets too much time go by, and they can get sidetracked. Give them constant feedback on what they're doing well, what they need to improve on, and what metrics they are hitting. They also appreciate blunt and direct feedback, versus vague comments or beating around the bush. They thrive on knowing how they are doing. They're asking, what can I do better? I have found with my team that constant, clear feedback is important.

So is training. Across all organizations and industries, roughly 70 percent of every organization's dollar is spent on payroll, but only about 1 percent is spent on training. This future workforce craves training. You may find younger workers who are truly A-players, but a lot of them are young and may be a B-player who can improve greatly with proper training and coaching. That doesn't mean you have to spend a lot of money on seminars and consultants. If you boost your training budget from 1 percent to 3 percent, that can make a big difference.

But the most cost-effective way to train someone is to just give them your time. Somebody has to be there to hold them accountable and teach them and mentor them. Even if it's just fifteen minutes a week, or if it's fifteen minutes every two weeks, it's better than nothing. If you're not in the position to mentor them personally, match another mentor with the person, maybe a senior Nurse Practitioner who's been with the company for twenty years to mentor your new NP who's only been on the job for two years. The mentor should be somebody that this person wants to become. They can ask questions—hey, I'm struggling with this. What should I do? How should I handle this? What did you do at this point in your career?

This workforce also wants you to get out of their way. Give them the autonomy and flexibility to make decisions, make mistakes, and execute. Coach them through the mistakes and be sure to praise them when they hit their numbers. I think one of the best management tips is to catch somebody doing really great things. Praise them in front of a lot people. Acknowledge their good work, because they want to become an expert in their field.

A lot of people don't want to do all this. But there's a big payoff to it. Theodore Roosevelt has a famous quote: "No one cares how much you know, until they know how much you care." I think this workforce has to see that you care for them as a person, perhaps more than you care about the results. You hold them accountable and you're clear with them, but with any type of leadership or coaching or mentoring there has to be care for the individual above what they can do for you. Because if they sniff out that you really care only about what they can do for you, their level of engagement goes way down. But if they can sense that their boss or direct report really cares about them as a person and about what's going on in their life, they're way, way more likely to do a great job and stay in the position.

Three Questions to Ask

In a leadership role, the leader should ask these three questions:

1. What went well this past week?

2.   What went wrong in the past week?

3.   How can I help you?

Those three questions will sift out where the team member needs help from a mentor or more training.

3. SHOW A PATH FOR GROWTH.

If you're hiring people who are coachable, driven, and people-savvy, they want to grow. These are A-players. They don't just show up for a paycheck. These people constantly want a challenge.

For retention, you're going to have to create challenges and anticipate how to help this person progress year to year, three years from now and five years from now. If they don't get that challenge, they're going to leave. If they feel like they have been doing the same thing for three years, they are gone. They're looking for something else.

Ideally, you should create some sort of growth plan, one that has an increase in title, an increase in money, and in increase in responsibility, over time. If you can't do those three things all at once every couple years, then you can offer one or two of those things. If you can't do any of those three things, come up with some other creative ways to advance their responsibility. Maybe ask them to sit on an advisory board or committee, if you can't give them a true title, money, or responsibility changes.

Make it clear that these changes are merit-based, and that not everybody gets them. These are earned, which makes it more valuable. If you just give a growth position to everybody who hits the one-year mark or the two-year mark, it becomes fake and it actually works against you. It has to be for those people who are going the extra mile. That motivates them to do more, continue to learn, and continue to push themselves into a growth mentality versus a static mentality.

If you've got a bunch of static employees who are complacent, your company is not going to grow and you're going to be static as well.

If you've got a bunch of static employees who are complacent, your company is not going to grow and you're going to be static as well. But because you're hiring go-getters, those true team players, they don't want that. They want an organization where people are constantly learning, growing, and getting better.

For example, we have three core values. The first: We deliver. The second: We serve. And the third: We get better every day. That means that, at our core, we are not a static organization. We're constantly asking ourselves the question, "how can I improve today?" What's the one thing I can do better today? We're pushing ourselves out of our comfort zone to learn. You want to create a team that does that, too.

Within our staff, we have recruiters who start off as search associates. They can move up to search consultant, then search director, then director of recruitment, and finally VP of operations. With each step comes more money and more responsibility, along with a title change. If you're working in a human resources department, maybe somebody starts out as a human resources assistant right out of college, and then moves to an HR consultant, then an HR manager, then a director of HR. That doesn't mean everybody's going to move through those roles. But in the recruiting process and again in the retention process, if the candidate sees that there's a growth progression, then they're more likely to join your organization and stay there. They need to see that they can grow here, that they can have a long-term career, that they can stay for ten or twenty years, make a huge impact, and eventually have a chance to become a director of the company.

They also know they might get passed up for a promotion, but just knowing that there is a growth plan that you've created and that it's not guaranteed puts them into a position of wanting to be up for the challenge. Those real team players will jump all over that. They want to join and stay in an organization that has challenges and rewards in store for them. The fact that you've carved out a growth plan is huge.

I know that this is not as easy in some professions. If you've been trained for a specialized position, like Nurse Practitioner, what else can you aspire to? That's where creativity is especially important. Perhaps you put them on a medical director team or a board of directors, or you create a committee of senior level Nurse Practitioners or some sort of think tank, where they are part of the big picture and they're making decisions for the organization. Maybe you make mentoring younger NPs part of a growth plan. Or put them on a path where they're managing other RNs and NPs. Each step ideally has a change in title, responsibility, and salary. Maybe they become a senior Nurse Practitioner or vice president of operations, Nurse Practitioner division. They might still be doing their core job as a primary care Nurse Practitioner, but now they're part of committees or adding responsibilities, they're mentoring, they're teaching, and there's some sort of pay increase with that.

Now, a lot of nurses don't want to have anything to do with management. They might be happy with just doing primary care as an NP. In that case, you can try to tailor the growth plan to their interests. For instance, if they are working in primary care, but they really have an interest in diabetes education, you help them get their diabetes educator certificate. They go to school for it, they form a committee, they do some teaching, they do "lunch and learn" meetings with the rest of the Nurse Practitioners. It's about getting inside their head and figuring out what their passion is and how you can fuel that passion. You also need to think ahead about what's next for this person, what's going to keep them challenged, and how you can retain this person, especially if they are an A-player. What initiative do I have to put in place to keep them versus sitting on my hands and saying, it is what it is, it's a primary care NP job, and hope they stay here for twenty years. That's taking a very passive approach, and that's how turnover happens. The reality is, they're going to get bored and they're going to move on.

AN EXAMPLE OF SHOWING A PATH FOR GROWTH

"I have a current APP who has shown an interest in providing palliative care and becoming the lead medical provider for our hospital's palliative care team. I have encouraged her to apply and have written a strong letter of recommendation for her entrance into the University of Washington's Palliative Care training program. She will receive time off to complete the education and time to perform these duties. For the hospital, this small investment will bring a great return."

Karen Geheb, MD, CMD

Director of Hospitalist Services

Pullman Regional Hospital

4. GIVE THEM A VOICE

This one is so easy to apply, and it's so powerful. This is such a hot button for the younger future workforce. They want to join an organization that hears their voice. They become excited about it. They want to be a part of the big picture and take part in where the organization is going, and they want you to hear them. Some of the best ideas you get are going to come from them, but that doesn't mean you have to implement all of their ideas. They know this. They don't expect all of their ideas to be used. But just the fact that you're hearing their voice and there's a chance you may take their ideas creates huge buy-in. It doesn't cost much money. It does take up some time, but it's an easy implementation with profound rewards in terms of retention.

At NP Now, we hold quarterly offsite meetings. Every three months, we sit down as a team and break out into groups. In these groups, we ask: What's working? What's broken? What's confusing? And they answer. They ask those in management other questions. What in our organization is working? What's broken? What's not working? What's confusing?

They write it all out and brainstorm. When they get to the end, they figure out some themes, some commonalities that they're all saying, and then they present it to the group. Everyone in all the groups hears what each of the groups is saying. As a leadership team, we're listening to everything that's said, and then we figure out what we need to implement.

Sometimes, we'll try to answer the question right there: Since everybody's talking about thing x that we need to improve—say it's a certain process—let's kick it around right here and talk about it. Then it becomes a company-wide discussion, or at least the leaders of those groups are discussing how we improve those processes. This not only can generate some of your best ideas, but it also gives your younger workforce a voice. It's collaborative, which they love. Then, when you make decisions based on their voice, the level of buy-in is so much higher. They feel like they had a significant role in changing the direction of the practice. Now they're saying, "Hey, I'm affecting the organization. My organization has a big vision, it has a strong core purpose, and it's doing some really good, cool things in the community—and I'm having an impact in that."

We also hold meetings individually. You can include this when holding leadership meetings and accountability meetings every week or two. Ask them what they think the company needs to start doing, stop doing, and keep doing. It's a different version of those questions, but it's another way to let them express their voice. This younger workforce is very tech-savvy. They can find information fast. They're creative. They think outside the box. Asking them the questions will generate some of your best ideas, if you only listen to them and they feel like they are genuinely being listened to.

Another cool thing I've heard about some companies doing is creating an email address where people can send their ideas. I haven't tried it, but I've heard it can be effective. Somebody in leadership needs to check the email regularly and respond thoughtfully. Then you not only have a constant flow of new ideas but you are continually reinforcing the notion that your workers' voices are being heard.

When we interview NPs and PAs, especially the members of this new future workforce, you can really sense their excitement once we talk about how their voice is going to make a difference.

CREATE A CHAMPIONSHIP COMPANY CULTURE.

These four things must be implemented to some degree right away. If you cannot implement them all at once, take them in baby steps. Even if you can implement just a little bit of all four of these strategies, do it now. Then talk about it in the recruitment process and hammer it home to your workforce to build retention.

Add these to your attraction-based job description so recruits can see it on paper. Talk to them about it during the interview and hiring process. Constantly hit on these four things. If they hear these four things during the recruitment process, then I can guarantee you that you're putting yourself at a huge advantage in landing these people and keeping them long term.

As NPs, PAs, physicians, and other medical providers become harder and harder to find, and the demand for them increases, you'll have such a competitive advantage if you talk about these four things during the recruitment and retention process. But it is critical that you actually deliver on them. Because if you don't deliver, they are going to figure it out fast. If they think it was just smoke and mirrors, they will end up leaving after six months or a year, because you're just like all the other organizations.

But if you stress these points constantly and actually walk the walk, now not only are you going to attract the A-players, but your retention is also going to go through the roof. Just imagine what that will do for your organization as far as revenue, patient satisfaction, patient access, and company culture. The cost of turnover is too high to not take this seriously.

Being able to retain great people is an enormous competitive advantage.

CONCLUSION

The working world is more stressful than ever these days. Everyone is striving to do more work with fewer workers. Resources are scarce, but the work keeps piling up. This has resulted in some pretty toxic work environments.

There is blame. There is finger pointing. There is chaos. It is up to us to correct this situation by creating a solid company culture. I think we owe it to the people who work on our team to have a healthy work environment.

We owe it to the people who work on our team to have a healthy work environment.

We all come from families that are in some way unhealthy or dysfunctional. It varies by degree, but most families create at least a little stress. The world today, at almost every level, is unpredictable and chaotic. I think we owe it to ourselves and to the world to create as stable, predictable, and healthy a work environment as we possibly can—an environment in which people can feel safe, they can feel heard, and they can feel like they're part of something great.

If you really want to build a world-class team, and you know that it will have to be made up largely of this future workforce, I believe you need to capitalize on the strategies that I have offered in this book. My attraction-based recruiting model applies to anybody that you're hiring, from the CEO to a doctor or nurse to maintenance staff. All of it can and should be applied to all of them. But specifically with the medical providers, the people that are really hard to find and land, you don't have a choice. Like I said earlier: adjust or lose. When physicians, RNs, NPs, and PAs have so many options, and as they become more in demand, you must position your organization to look nothing like your competitors so that they choose to join you.

The strategies that I've brought up in this book will help you differentiate yourself so that you're running so far ahead of the pack that A-players can clearly see that your organization and your company culture is so different that they want to join you. Even if you're a smaller company that doesn't have all the bragging rights that a bigger company may have, you need to capitalize on your strengths, sell those strengths, implement these practices, and push these hot buttons that this future workforce is looking for.

It starts with creating an irresistible company culture. That's what this younger workforce is looking for. They're looking for real and authentic. So even if you do not have the fanciest website or the plushest office, at your core you are authentic and real. You have a passion.

The future workforce craves real and authentic.

You have a heart. You truly believe in what you are doing. This younger workforce can sniff that out. They can sniff out "fake" even faster. So be true to who you are, and let that come out in the recruitment, hiring, and retention process. They're more likely to join and stay with an organization that lives its core purpose, core values, and vision.

APPENDIX A:
CIS FORM

This is the information our clients require when we present them with a resume, also it better helps us match you with future job openings. We will not be able to submit you as a candidate until we receive this document back from you so please complete and e-mail back to me a.s.a.p. This information will give you a better opportunity of getting an interview in a timely fashion.

Name: _____

Additional Contact information:

    □ Work phone #: _____

    □ Cell #: _____

    □ Home email: _____

    □ Work email: _____

Describe your ideal position: _____

_____

What is the main reason for looking for a new position?

_____

_____

Current Compensation Outline: (Companies will verify these amounts so be as exact as possible.)

- Base: _____

- Bonus Potential: _____

- Bonus earned last year: _____

What are you looking for in total compensation?

_____

How far do you currently commute to work?

_____

Willing to relocate?

- If yes, where? _____

- If not, how many minutes are you willing to commute from home for the right position? _____

Why do you think you would be good for this position?

_____

_____

Describe your job search activity in the last 6 months, did you receive any offers?

_____

_____

Hobbies/interests away from work:

_____

_____

Do you have a non-compete or reimbursement clause for tuition or relocation assistance?

_____

_____

HOT BUTTON QUESTIONS:

(These are the areas the employer has designated as critical to the success of this position, please answer each question as thoroughly as possible)

1. Describe your experience in primary care: _____

   _____

2. What is your most recent exposure to chronic adult primary care patients:

   _____

   _____

3. Explain your strengths as a Nurse Practitioner in primary care: _____

_____

As part of the NP Now process, one of the things we do to give you a "leg up" on any other candidates that may be considered for this position is to gather informal reference checks at the beginning of the process. Please provide us with the names and email addresses of just 2 people you would be comfortable with us contacting today about your professional background.

DISCLOSURE STATEMENT

I understand that NP Now may conduct a reference and education check. This reference may include information regarding character, work record, general knowledge and capabilities, and reputation. I hereby acknowledge that I have read and understand this statement, and hereby authorize NP Now to obtain a reference check as described above.

Name/Electronic Signature: _____

BUSINESS REFERENCES

Name: _____

Email address: _____

Brief Summary of Relationship between Candidate and Reference: _____

Name: _____

Email address: _____

Brief Summary of Relationship between Candidate and Reference: _____

_____

APPENDIX B

For more information contact:

Katie Ozburn

NP Now, LLC

P: 843.574.8234

katie@npnow.com

Progressive health-care organization seeks a Nurse Practitioner to work in an outpatient psych setting in the Lafayette, Indiana area!

This NP will have the opportunity to be a part of a group that lives and breathes a commitment to the community, a commitment to being involved and to being that extra hand patients and families need while they recover from mental health/psychiatry disease!

Company:

- Progressive Healthcare Organization that believes in treating the "whole person" integrating physical, mental and social well-being to help people achieve their optimum health.

- For over 40 years this Organization has been serving their community and are accredited by the Joint Commission and certified by the Indiana Division of Mental Health and Addictions.

- Providing the highest level of patient care, this organization is committed to meeting the needs of their community through outreach into the community, including advocacy, events and educational opportunities.

- Last year alone they served over 32,000 patients in over 46 counties across Indiana.

- Highly value their providers and staff; the $128.8 Million in revenue generated this past year, over $56 million is dedicated to their employees' salaries and benefits.

Benefits and Features:

- $95,000-$120,000/year in salary, depending on experience

- Full medical benefits, Dental, Vision, Life, 401K

- Excellent PTO package; 3 weeks

Your Role with the Company:

- M-F flexible schedule, no call

- APRN (Advanced Practice RN)/ MSN / FNP-BC, Family Nurse Practitioner will have great support in a collegial team setting seeing patients in a mental health capacity

- Nurse Practitioner will identify behavioral health issues, collaborating with psychiatrists and other Nurse Practitioners

- APRN/MSN/AGNP/FNP/PNP can see either just adults or just children.

- Candidate would need to build rapport well and provide patient focused/customer service care

Background Profile:

- FNP/Family Nurse Practitioner, APRN, Nurse Practitioner, AGNP, PMHMP, Psych Nurse Practitioner

- 6+ months of experience in a psych setting, as an NP or RN

- Open to a new graduate PMHNP

TESTIMONIALS

"NP NOW cannot be recommended enough. Whether you are new graduate or experienced healthcare provider, you WILL find a position to your liking. As a new graduate using this exceptional recruiting company, I was able to have an interview and a solid offer within 2 weeks of applying. They are professional, timely and courteous. Best of all, NP NOW does not SELL you a position. They make sure YOU, the provider is happy with the process and the position. NP NOW is HIGHLY recommended."

—Nurse Practitioner

"I cannot tell you how happy I am . This is truly a great thing. I have been waiting for a position like this for years. My years of hard work paid off, and finally I am being recognized for it. I am so thankful to you. I cannot thank you enough."

—Nurse Practitioner

"David Wolfe was excellent in helping me land my new job. He returned every call, email and text on a timely manner. He advocated very well for me as an NP seeking a new job. I highly recommend him if you are seeking to hire or find an NP job."

—Margie S.

"Great help in communication and linking me to my new position."

—Mike Wallace

"David Wolfe helped me navigate the arduous process of attaining a new NP position. Overall, a great experience."

—Kim Huck

"David is an excellent recruiter. He is diligent and I had a great experience working with him."

—Delenie Wong

"My time with David was worth it! I'm glad I contacted him 'cause the end result was awesome! Yay!!!"

—Graceolayinka Akinpetide

"David Wolfe was very helpful and wonderful to work with."

—Cassie Pratt

If you want us to be your "secret weapon" and make you look great to your organization by building you a world-class NP or PA team, contact us at:

NP Now—The Nurse Practitioner Search Firm

sales@npnow.com

843.574.8244

www.npnow.com

www.ingramcontent.com/pod-product-compliance
Lightning Source LLC
Jackson TN
JSHW011410130125
77033JS00024B/953